HIDDEN RICHES

by H. Romaine Stauffer

Christian Light Publications, Inc.
Harrisonburg, Virginia 22801
1983

ISBN 0-87813-520-0

Contents

Introduction

The freedom and comfort which Mennonites in North America enjoy is generally taken for granted. If we ever knew what it cost our forefathers to come to this land, we have forgotten. Many of us do not even know the first names of our ancestors who braved the Atlantic and transplanted in North America the Mennonite and Amish surnames of Good, Martin, Landis, High, Stoltzfus, Miller, Stauffer, King, and many others.

We need to be reminded of the persecution and suffering of our forefathers which bought for us the peace and freedom we enjoy today. We have no promise we may not someday face similar conditions. One of the ways we can prepare for the suffering we may have to endure is to be familiar with experiences of our forefathers and how they remained faithful to God under terrible pressures and difficulties. We, today, are so accustomed to having the precious freedom they risked their lives to find. It has made us comfortable and sometimes lazy in our faith. Many times we have lost the will to fight against the temptations of the world. Mennonites are losing at an alarming rate the basic principles on which their faith was built in the Reformation. We do not value our faith as highly as did those who looked death in the eye to have it.

I have written this story for two reasons: (1) That we might know the high price our forefathers paid for their faith, and (2) That we might appreciate the faith and freedom we enjoy and hold it fast.

Naturally, when studying history, one is drawn to research his personal history. While I have chosen to tell the story of my ancestors, the Christian Burkholder family, their experiences are typical of many other Swiss and German families who came to America in the years between 1700 and 1755.

The story is based on historical facts. Where facts were not available, fiction has supplied details to give body to the story. The fictional parts have many times been taken from old books recounting the experiences of other persons. While they may not have happened to the Burkholder family exactly as stated, they are typical of what others experienced

v

and may just as well have happened to the Burkholders.

Much of the information found in the Epilogue is taken from the "Burkholder Roots" section of the *Daniel S. Burkholder Family History,* published by Amos B. Hoover in 1981. As a researcher, he has found and written much of the information known about the Christian Burkholder family. This material has been used with his permission.

Amos B. Hoover has in his possession the *Martyrs Mirror* which Christian Burkholder bought in 1761. This book was lost for over a century and was discovered in 1980. In addition to being a priceless family heirloom, it is as well an authoritative document of family history. In his own hand, Christian wrote several pages of data, setting the record straight on some incorrect names and dates which were ignorantly published before then. Spelling, however, was not so important then and inconsistencies are not to be taken seriously. Christian himself used five different spellings to record the name *Burkholder* six times. His own name he recorded as "Chrystli," indicating he may have been called by that name as a child to distinguish him from his father. The English translation of the name would be "Christy."

From old books such as these we have been able to learn the Christian Burkholder family came to Pennsylvania in 1754. The *Strassbarger Hinke* ship list recorded the signatures of 29,758 people who came to Philadelphia. Among these, in the year 1754, we find the names of the three Burkholder boys arriving Tuesday, October 1, 1754 on the ship *Phoenix,* John Spurrier being the captain. Christian's writing on the ship list is identical to that found in his *Martyrs Mirror.* The names of the women and girls were not included.

It is my hope and prayer this story will help my children to appreciate their forefathers and the faith that has been passed down to them; and further, that children of other surnames who read it will identify with their ancestors and appreciate their struggles, which very likely were quite similar. May they determine, as did Christian, to stand for the faith. As he wrote in his *Martyrs Mirror* below the name of his youngest child: Gott allein di ehr (to God alone be the honor).

Acknowledgements

I owe much to the many people who aided me in the writing of this book. I need, first of all, to thank my husband, Leroy, for his patience and willingness to listen as I shared with him the things I learned in the research for writing this story. Without his cooperation and support, this book could not have been written. My thanks is also extended to my five children, ranging in age from 14 to 2 years, for their patience with me and doing without the extras they might have had if I had not been using my time to write this book.

My parents, Lester and Betty (Burkholder) Burkholder, also deserve recognition for their help and support of my efforts. Their trip to Gerolsheim and the old Burkholder home in 1980 fanned the spark of interest in my heritage into the blaze which resulted in the writing of this book. Both of my parents are descendants of Christian Burkholder by different branches of the family tree.

I am also indebted to Amos B. Hoover for his help and advice. He loaned old and rare books to me for my research. One of these was a copy of the extremely rare book, *Journey to Pennsylvania in the Year 1750 and Return to Germany in the Year 1754,* written by Gottlieb Mittleberger. This book is a firsthand report of conditions at sea, cost of passage, and reports of Pennsylvania as it existed at that time. The book was an invaluable aid in writing this story.

HIDDEN RICHES

And I will give thee
the treasures of darkness,
and hidden riches
of secret places,
that thou mayest know
that I, the LORD,
which call thee by thy name,
am the God of Israel.
Isaiah 45:3

Chapter 1

Pennsylvania!

"Come back here," Christian ordered Buttercup, the most troublesome goat of the flock. Buttercup paid no attention. With a sigh, Christian got up to chase the annoying goat back to the others. Sometimes he wondered if he would herd goats for the rest of his life. The job had once been his brother Ulrich's. Then it was passed on to Peter and now to Christian. It wasn't that he really minded herding goats. It was a good job for a six-year-old boy. He loved to be outdoors and some of the goats were his best friends. It was just at times when Buttercup or one of the other goats got a stubborn streak that Christian wished he were old enough to do field work. But since he was the youngest in the family, he was likely to be stuck with the job for a long time.

Buttercup seemed to think the chase was a game. She led Christian up and down the gently rolling German Palatinate hills, keeping just out of his

reach. At last he got close enough to give her a whack across the hindquarters with his forked stick. Buttercup turned and headed toward home. Christian followed in hot pursuit through the cobblestone streets of the little farming village of Gerolsheim. Buttercup charged through the open gate of the fence which surrounded the Burkholder family farm buildings and headed into the courtyard. This was home, not only to Christian's family, but also to his uncle, Abraham Burkholder, and his family, as well as Grandfather, Hans Burkholder.

Christian skidded to a stop as he rounded the corner of the house. Grandfather was sitting on a chair under the tree in the courtyard eating some of the cherries Peter had just picked from a fallen branch of the overloaded cherry tree. Buttercup stood there calmly eating the leaves from the branch as though that was why she had come home in the first place.

Christian grabbed the bell rope around Buttercup's neck and switched her as he led her away to the goat stall across the courtyard. Then he ran back to see Grandfather. Christian had not known Grandfather was back in Gerolsheim. He had been on a trip to give communion to some of the five German Swisser* churches over which he was bishop. It was good to see him again.

Christian stepped over the handles of the wooden rake and pitchfork his oldest sisters, Barbara and Anna, had dropped when they came in from helping Ulrich make hay. He sat down on the edge of the

---

*The name *Mennonite* was not used in Germany at this time. They were known as *Swissers* rather than Mennonites.

well beside Anna and slowly sipped the glass of water she dipped from a bucket Barbara had just brought up from the cool depths below. He could see his mother and sister, both named Elizabeth, preparing supper through the open doorway of their ordinary, German, half-timbered house. The outer walls of the house were made of vertical and horizontal timbers which framed spaces filled with stone and mortar masonary. The brown timbers contrasted pleasantly with the cream-colored wall.

Grandfather took another handful of cherries from the bowl Peter held out to him. He continued speaking to Father, who sat on a log nearby, looking thoughtfully at a letter in his lap.

"I see the whole congregation here will never be able to agree to all go at once as I hoped," Grandfather was saying. "Those who want to go will have to go as it suits them. But I have waited too long. I am too old now to make such a trip. Yet I am sure it is the right thing to do. I remember my father, Hans, often telling how he was persecuted in Switzerland. Twice he was in prison and escaped. Then he was driven from home and came here to Germany. I was still very young when Mother brought me and my six brothers and sisters here to be with Father in 1671. I will never forget that long walk from Switzerland to Germany.

"My father hoped Germany would be a place where we could worship God in peace and live according to our beliefs. It is true we are not burned at the stake and beheaded as they were in Switzerland, but you know how it is. The government is still trying to get rid of us. They make us pay such high taxes we have hardly anything left. We pay extra taxes so our young men do not have to join the army. We pay extra taxes to bury our dead. They don't let us marry or pass our belongings on to our children without going through a long legal process and great expense. Even with paying these taxes, we are almost considered outlaws because we will not help fight Germany's wars. We are not able to teach anyone but our own children our faith without danger and trouble. The freedom my father wanted is not found here."

"This letter from Daniel Groff surely makes Pennsylvania sound good," Father agreed. "He says the government there touches them so lightly they hardly feel it. He promises to help us find a home if we want to come."

"We have often talked of going to Pennsylvania," Grandfather repeated. "Others have gone and have found good land. I will not live much longer. I shall never leave Germany. But you can go, Christian. You have these boys, Ulrich, Peter, and little Christli to think of. In Pennsylvania they could grow up free to believe the Bible and practice it without all these restrictions of the state. I wish you would go before the boys are any older."

Young Christian leaned forward eagerly to hear what Father would say. He had often heard Father and Grandfather talk of going to Pennsylvania, but this time Grandfather was serious. He really wanted them to go.

Father remained silent. At last he said slowly, "We will pray and ask God to tell us His will. I am a minister. I cannot just walk away and leave my church without a shepherd. But you are right. I must think of the boys, too. I will make the decision

13

to go or stay as the Lord tells me."

"Yah, that is the only way," Grandfather agreed, stroking his white beard. "I will pray, too, that He will tell you. Now I must go lie down."

Leaning heavily on his walking stick, Grandfather got stiffly to his feet and started toward his room.

Chapter 2

A Private Conversation

"Christli," Ulrich called his little brother, "take these eggs in to Mother."

Christian gave his favorite goat, Primrose, a final pat, picked up the basket of eggs, and headed for the house. The house seemed dark in comparison to the bright sunshine outside. Christian stood in the doorway a minute, waiting for his eyes to adjust to the dim light. He could not help hearing his father speaking to Mother in the next room.

"I just can't get it from my mind, Elizabeth. Just before he passed away, Grandfather became convinced we should go. I have waited and prayed more than a year now, seeking the Lord's will. I am more sure all the time Grandfather was right. Germany continually seems either to be involved in wars herself or in the path of other countries at war. A new war could break out any time again. Ulrich is soon of draft age. Will we be able to pay the high war tax it will take to keep him from being forced into the army?"

Standing in the doorway, Christian sucked in his breath. Father and Mother were talking again about going to Pennsylvania! He knew he should not be listening, but he felt he just *had* to know if Father had decided to go or not. He leaned against the doorway and listened as Mother answered.

"I know, Christian. Grandfather Burkholder was right when he said peace and freedom are not to be found for us in Germany. The reports from Pennsylvania are almost too good to be true. But Pennsylvania is a long ways from here. There is so much danger on the trip. Many ships have been robbed by pirates or lost in storms at sea. So many of the people who leave Germany never get to Pennsylvania at all. There is so much sickness on the ships that it is rare for a family to get there without at least one of the family dying at sea. The children are often the ones who suffer most and die. Would it be right to risk losing Christli or any of the others for Ulrich's sake?"

"That is a hard question, Elizabeth. But suppose we do stay here. Times are hard because of the high taxes, wars, and cattle diseases. Our Mennonite brothers in Holland are not able to give enough help for all the poor here. We are getting more poor every year. Before long we will be so poor we will not be able to think of going even if we want to. In a few years Peter and Christli will also be of draft age. They, too, will be persecuted for being non-resistant Anabaptists. And we will need to pay two more high taxes for them. In Pennsylvania we would be able to make a decent living and at the same time be free to live according to our beliefs without being bothered by the government. If we are going to go next spring, we must soon decide so we can get ready in time."

"Yah well, Christian. We will do what God has told you. If He has said we should go, I will not insist we stay."

"Surely if God wants us to go, He can see that we get there safely," Father said. "Let's pray together now and ask Him to tell us if our wishes are not His will."

Christian heard a muffled thump which told him his parents had dropped to their knees to pray. He would not listen to this sacred conversation. Softly he set the basket of eggs on the table and tiptoed from the house as he heard Father begin speaking earnestly to God.

As he stepped out into the bright sunshine again, Christian wondered if they really would go to Pennsylvania next spring. Although Father had talked of it so often, he had never said "next spring" as he had today. Would God say, "Go"? If He did, an exciting summer lay ahead of them. But Christian felt a little afraid too. Mother thought he might die before he got to Pennsylvania.

This was too big and wonderful to tell anyone, Christian decided. He would not even tell Peter, although he and Peter usually shared everything. Breathless with a strange mixture of excitement and fear, Christian ran back to his goats. He was sure Ulrich would ask what had kept him so long. But Ulrich had gone back to his own work and Christian was left alone to ponder his secret.

Chapter 3

An Important Decision

"Christli, how would you like to go to Pennsylvania?" Father asked suddenly one noon as he drained the last of the milk from his bowl of potato soup.

Christian's eyes widened and stared over the edge of his bread and goat's cheese.

"Why? Are we going?" he asked without answering Father's question. He looked quickly at the circle of faces around the table. Only his mother's face gave the answer.

"Yes, we are planning to go, the Lord willing," Father answered. "Grandfather wanted us to to go. Mother and I have prayed about it, and it seems the Lord wants us to go, too. I have written to Daniel Groff in Pennsylvania telling him of our decision. Unless something happens to stop us, we will plan to start next spring."

Next spring! It was October now. Only the winter months lay between now and the start of a wonderful adventure. The rest of the family was silent, each busy with his own thoughts. But all the questions Christian had been collecting since he first overheard his parents discussing the trip, spilled out in a torrent.

"Father, can I take Primrose along? Will we see any Indians? Is anyone else we know going with us?"

"I don't know the answers to all those questions yet," Father laughed when Christian stopped for breath. "We will find the answers as we go along. I do know the Jacob Frey family is planning to go with us."

Christian's eagerness and excitement loosened the tongues of the others. They began discussing plans and Christian listened with both ears. He was glad Jacob Freys would go with them. Their son, Martin, was just a year younger than Christian. Martin's brother, Hans, was eleven, one year older than Peter. They were already good friends. The Frey's two older girls were near Elizabeth's age. It would be nice to have others with them their own age.

Father said it was best to begin the trip in the spring. From what others who had made the trip had told him, they could expect to spend six months traveling. If they left Gerolsheim in April, they should reach Pennylvania sometime in October. Most of the things they owned here would have to be sold. They would need the money to pay for the ocean fare and costs of traveling.

They could have stayed around the table much longer, discussing and wondering about the future. But this day could not be wasted either. Mother began gathering the dishes for washing as Father headed for the barn. Christian followed, his mind busy. For the first time, he realized going to Pennsylvania would mean leaving and never returning to the only home he had ever known.

Christian looked back at his mother, aunt, and sisters—busy in the familiar kitchen—as if seeing it for the first time. Every corner of the room held precious memories. Did he really want to leave the dear, familiar rooms of this home for a place he had never seen? He stood in the doorway a moment, looking at the small cluster of houses that was Gerolsheim and the mountains in the distance beyond. Would the people there be as friendly and comfortable to live with as their family and friends here? Would there be such beautiful mountains in Pennsylvania?

Already Christian felt a twinge of homesickness cross over his heart when he thought of leaving behind all the things he had known and loved. But in an instant he remembered Father had often said, "God never takes away a good thing without giving something better." These reassuring words comforted him strangely. Father had asked God if they should go to Pennsylvania. God and Father could not both be wrong. This home in Germany may have been good, but the one they would find in Pennsylvania must be better.

Taking big steps, Christian carefully placed his feet in the prints Father's big leather boots had made in the mud, and followed him across the courtyard to the barn. Whether to a barn in Germany or to a home in Pennsylvania, Christian was ready to follow his father.

20

Chapter 4

Plans

A sudden blast of cold air swept into the room ahead of Father. He quickly pushed the door shut behind him and waved a letter at the twelve pairs of eyes turned toward him from his own family and his brother Abraham's family.

"Good news!" Father exclaimed. "We have a letter from Daniel Groff in Pennsylvania. He urges us to come and offers to help pay our way if we don't have enough money. There seems to be nothing now to stop us from going to Pennsylvania this spring. We will begin right away to sell the things we can't take with us and get ready to go. This is already the end of January. I hope we will be ready to leave by the end of March. Can you be ready to leave by then, Elizabeth?"

"I will be ready whenever you are," Mother said quietly. Her eyes met Father's and then traveled around the room as though lightly caressing each of her possessions and relatives, bidding them good-by. Her gaze stopped on little Christian's eager, upturned face.

"So Christli is to have his wish," Mother said, the twinkle in her voice matching the one in her eyes. "He will go on a big ship across the ocean and maybe see some Indians in Pennsylvania."

Christian felt his face grow warm with embarrassment. He nodded his head and bent low over the pair of leather boots he had been rubbing with lard to waterproof them. His long hair fell forward far enough to partly hide his face, but his eager ears caught every word as he listened to Father and Uncle Abraham discussing which things could be taken along and which must be left behind.

It really is true! Christian thought. They were no longer saying "if" we go, but "when" we go. The trip which they had talked of making ever since he could remember was no longer "sometime." It was now.

"We will need to take our iron pans and ladles. I should take seeds to start a garden and, of course, herbs and teas for medicines," Mother was saying. "We will want to take as much food as we can to eat along the way."

"I will need my ax, shovel, and saw," Father added. "And it would be good to take rye and barley seed if we have room. We will really need everything we have here, but we can't take it all. We will have to make do with very little at first.

"We have a lot of work to do between now and the end of March," Father continued. "I have six orders for baskets. I may as well get them out of the way. Christli, run out and get a bundle of strips for me. I had better weave baskets every evening I can until the orders are filled."

Christian brought the bundle of split-oak strips and laid them on the floor beside Father. He always liked to watch Father weave baskets. It took a lot of patience and skill to make a split-oak basket. But the baskets were very durable and lasted for many years. Most of Father's basket making was done on winter evenings like this. It was only a sideline to the farming which was his main occupation. He had begun making baskets simply because of his family's need for them. But word of his skill had spread and now he also made a few baskets for friends and neighbors.

Father used only white oak trees for basket making. His practiced eye judged the trees and chose only those he knew were perfect. The tree had to be young and not larger than ten inches around. It must have a straight trunk with no branches for the first ten or fifteen feet. When Father found such a tree, he chipped the trunk with his ax to see if the rings around the trunk were spaced properly. If the rings were too far apart or too close together, the wood did not split to the proper thickness for baskets. One good tree could be made into as many as thirty baskets.

After Father chose a tree, he felled it with his ax and cut it into logs according to the size of basket he intended to make. The larger the basket, the longer the logs needed to be. The logs were kept in a cool place so they would not dry too quickly. Green wood was much easier to work with than seasoned wood.

As he needed them, Father split the logs first in half and then into quarters. The inner part of the core was removed from each quarter. This triangular piece of wood was split several more times and shaved on the shnitzel-bunk to form the ribs, rim, and handle of the basket. The rim was shaped and soaked in water so it would keep its shape. The ribs were shaved to about one-sixteenth of an inch and fastened to the rim.

After the skeleton parts of the basket were made, the remaining quarter section of the log was again split several times. These splits were made carefully by working it against a brech-shtuck.* Depending on its size, the quarter section separated into three or four smaller splints.

From this point on, the work must be done exactly right. Each of the three or four splints were split into the thinner, more pliable strips to be used for the actual weaving. Father made a small slit with a knife at the top of the splint. Then he carefully peeled the splint into strips, one-half inch wide and only one-thirty-second of an inch thick. He worked slowly by hand, making sure the strips split evenly and did not tear at dry spots. When the thin strips were made, he shaved them smooth so they would not split when they were woven around the ribs of the basket.

Christian watched now as Father began to weave the thin strips into the skeleton of the basket he had begun the day before. Christian knew it was not as easy as it looked. He had tried to make a small basket. Even though he carefully followed Father's motions, his finished basket was lopsided and floppy.

Father dampened the strips with water so they

*A post in the barnyard.

24

would not break or split. He threaded a strip between two ribs and wove it up and down between the ribs all around the basket. He worked from the top towards the bottom, working the ends of the strips in so no nails or glue were needed to fasten them. Then he turned the basket over and did the same thing again; only this time he worked from the bottom to top. He stopped weaving when all but about two inches in the basket's middle was filled. Then he hung the basket near the fire. It would dry and shrink overnight. After it was drawn tightly together, he would fill the opening, which may widen to as much as three inches, and finish the weaving.

"I think I'll answer Daniel Groff's letter now," Father said when he had hung the basket near the fire. "I'll tell him to expect us in Philadelphia in September or October. I believe I will also write to Dirk Peters in Rotterdam. We will probably stop there or at Amsterdam before crossing the North Sea to England. I would like to see him if we are in Rotterdam."

Father sat at the table near a candle to write the letters. In the stillness, punctuated by the scratching of Father's quill pen, Christian picked up a split-oak strip and wound it around his finger. His mind was miles away from Gerolsheim and baskets.

What was Rotterdam like? And Philadelphia? What all might they see along the Rhine River? For a boy who had never been far from his own village, there was no end to the new questions and thoughts. Christian itched to leave, and yet dreaded it in a way. He knew once they left Gerolsheim, life would never be the same again.

Chapter 5

An Unexpected Farewell

Christian soon discovered the change in their lives had begun with the arrival of Daniel Groff's letter. After that, there were few long, quiet winter evenings together around the fire. With all the work of planning and preparing for the trip, in addition to the usual daily chores, Mother seemed to fly about all day. She emptied chests and cupboards, packing and repacking things in their trunk and trying to decide what they could most easily do without.

They were using the same wooden trunk Grandfather's family used when they had moved from Switzerland to Germany. It was not much bigger than a small chest. Pieces of metal fitted over the corners to make them tight and strong. The beautifully-shaped metal hinges and clasps decorated the front of the chest and its flat lid. When the lid was closed and the leather straps fastened, a big key locked it securely. There was room for only the most necessary things. Father's *Froschauer* Bible and the *Ausbund* hymnbook were a must. And of course, they would take his hand tools, Mother's iron pans, and ticking to fill with feathers when they arrived. Mother planned to take a supply of yarn. She and the girls would pass their time knitting caps, mittens, and warm winter clothes while traveling. Winter would be on its way by the time they arrived in Pennsylvania.

Father was kept busy finding buyers for the tools, furniture, cow, goats, and sheep they would no longer need. He also had extra church work with the details of turning his ministry over to Christian Stauffer and Jacob Hirschler, and ordaining a new minister. It seemed to Christian he had been appointed full-time errand runner for everyone. The time they had hoped to be ready was only a few weeks away now.

Father was plagued with a sore arm. He had gotten a splinter in his finger when he was splitting a log into quarters for basket making. It was such a small thing at the time no one thought anything of it. But the wound refused to heal and began to fester. An angry red streak inched up his hand and towards his elbow. The doctor had come several times and cut the arm to let the bad blood out. The streak slowed its upward march temporarily, but then leaped above the elbow.

Father clamped his teeth as the doctor again made a cut. Cold sweat drenched his shirt. The pain was almost unbearable.

"I want you to stay in bed and rest," the doctor ordered. "Blood poisoning is not easily cured. I have done all I can. If the streak goes up any further . . .

well . . . I won't be able to help you. You must lie still and not move that arm at all."

How strange it seemed to have Father in bed during the daylight hours! Christian could not remember that ever happening before. Unspoken questions and fears set the whole family's nerves on edge. Many of their things were already sold. They could not think of leaving for Pennsylvania when Father was sick. If they were not going, Ulrich would need the tools to start the spring work soon. What should they do? Was God saying "stay" after all? The uncertainty of everything left them at a loss to know which way to turn. What if Father died? No one wanted to think of that.

Late one afternoon near the end of March, Mother sat by Father's bedside. She held his swollen hand in hers and watched his face. She thought he was sleeping. But in a moment his eyelids fluttered and he stirred.

"Elizabeth," Father said in a weak voice.

"Yes, Christian. I'm right here," Mother soothed.

"Elizabeth—I have been thinking—I don't believe—I shall live—much longer." Father could speak only a few words at a time.

"Oh, Christian! Don't talk like that. You will get well. You *must* get well," Mother's voice rose in desperation, and her eyes shimmered with tears.

"No. I am not going to get well," Father said haltingly with a note of resignation in his voice. "It seems the Lord wants me to live with Him instead of in Pennsylvania. If that is His will, I am content that it be so. But the children, Elizabeth. They must get to Pennsylvania. They will never be free to be nonresistant Swissers here in Germany. If you

28

promise to take them, even though I cannot go with you, I can die in peace. Will you promise?"

Exhausted from the effort of his long speech, Father closed his eyes. Mother's fears of the dangers of the trip were increased ten-fold to think of going without Father's strong shoulders to give her strength. She sat silently, struggling with her own fears at his request.

When she made no answer, Father opened his eyes and looked at her with pleading eyes. "It is my dying wish. The boys must have peace and freedom."

"Yes, Christian. I will take them," Mother promised, dropping to her knees beside the bed and burying her face in the feather tick.

Father reached out with his good hand and touched her shoulder. "God will go with you," he assured her. "I would like to see the children now. Will you call them?"

Mother nodded and wiped her eyes. Beginning with Barbara, who was twenty, and then on down the line to Anna, Ulrich, Elizabeth, Peter, and last of all, Christli, Father spoke a few parting words to each of his children. Ulrich, being the oldest son, would have to take his father's place though he was just seventeen years old. He came from Father's room bowed with sorrow and the weight of the task Father had placed on his shoulders.

When Peter came from Father's room, Mother motioned for Christian to come. He hung back a little, but finally walked hesitantly into the sickroom. The change that had come over his father in just a few weeks frightened Christian. Father's

illness seemed to be a threatening monster. Christian stood silently, just looking at his father's pain-racked body. Who would have thought a big, strong man like Father would be felled by a tiny splinter? It was so absurd. It couldn't be real! But it was.

"Christli is here," Mother said quietly.

Father opened his eyes. He reached for Christian's hand and squeezed it slightly.

"Christli," he said huskily, "be a good boy and do—what Mother—tells you. She will take you—to Pennsylvania. There you can—grow up strong and—free—to be a Swisser. And remember—who you are: Christian Burkholder."

"I will, Father, I will," Christian sobbed.

"God bless you—and keep you," Father whispered.

Blinded by tears, Christian stumbled out of the room and past his brothers and sisters huddled together outside the door. He had to be alone—somewhere—anywhere! Hardly knowing where his feet were taking him, he ran to the empty goat stall. He threw himself down on a pile of loose hay in the corner, sobbing as though his heart would break.

Chapter 6

Final Preparations

When Christian awoke one morning several days later, the house seemed unusually quiet. No early-morning sounds or smells greeted him. His heart stood still for a moment and then began pounding as fear returned. *Father! Did the stillness mean he was better or worse? Or did it mean——?*

Christian leaped out of bed, intending to run downstairs and find out. Then he hesitated. Did he want to know or not? He stood awkwardly on the cold floor, balancing himself first on one foot and then the other, trying to decide what to do.

"Christli," Barbara whispered from the other side of the door. "Christli, are you awake?"

"Yes," Christian whispered back.

"Put your better clothes on. We will be having company soon. Mother—wants to talk to you," Barbara choked as she turned away.

Mother was waiting for Christian outside his door. One look at her ashen face told him what he

32

feared was true.

"Christli, your father left us during the night," Mother said tenderly. "Ulrich has gone to tell the bishop. They will soon be back. Come. I want you to see Father before they get here."

Hand in hand, Christian and his mother stood at the side of the bed where Father's body lay. Christian reached out and touched Father's hand. Instantly, he drew back. An immense lump swelled and hardened in his throat. Father's hands which had always been warm, gentle, and kind, now lay cold, hard, and unmoving. The reality of what had happened hit him like a blow. "Father left us," Mother had said. Though his body lay on the bed, Father was gone. They would have to go on without him. Tears squeezed themselves past Christian's eyelids and trickled down his cheeks. Mother put her arm around his shoulders and led him gently from the room.

The next few days were a blur to Christian. It was a comfort to have Uncle Abraham's family in the house with them. A few close friends stopped by to offer their sympathy and encouragement. Everyone from their church came to the Burkholder home to attend their minister's funeral.

Christian sat quietly beside Peter all through the long, solemn service. Later, the family of seven slowly walked back home, leaving Father's body lying in a fresh grave only a few steps away from Grandfather's grave. Christian had no appetite for the customary meal following the funeral which was shared by all those who had attended.

Now that the uncertainty about Father was past, Mother picked up where he had left off and set about finishing his interrupted plans for going to Pennsylvania. Some well-meaning, but not very helpful, friends tried to convince her not to leave. Mother always kindly but firmly answered their protests by telling them she had promised Father she would go. It was his dying request and she was determined to keep her promise. They would be starting out a little later than Father had planned, but that could not be helped.

Ulrich wrote a letter to Daniel Groff, telling him of Father's death and of their expectations to arrive in the fall as planned. The last days at home were a flurry of activity. The last of the things they sold were taken away. The trunk was packed to the top and locked. Christian felt almost as though he was a stranger looking on at all these preparations and not actually a part of them. Even the pain of parting with Primrose was soon forgotten in the exciting round of preparations.

Mother had not gotten nearly enough money from the sale of their goods to pay the huge expense of taking the whole family across the ocean. But she would not think of leaving anyone behind as some families had done. They would all go together and trust the promises of God and Daniel Groff to see them through.

When Christian settled down for the night for the last time in the only home he had ever known, he lay awake a long time wondering about all the wonderful things that would begin to happen in the morning. He was so excited he didn't think he would sleep a wink all night.

Chapter 7

Good-bys

It seemed only a minute later when Christian felt his mother's hand on his shoulder shaking him gently as she whispered, "Christli, time to get up."

Christian sat up, yawned, and stretched. It was still very dark. He wondered why he was being awakened earlier than usual. But in a flash he remembered. *This was the day they were starting for Pennsylvania!*

Throwing back the feather tick, Christian slid out of the high featherbed to the floor and began dressing as fast as he could. Mother showed him a little cloth bag of money sewed inside the waistband of his breeches. She explained that each of them was wearing a little bag like this inside their clothing. It would be more safe than if one person carried all the money. He must be careful not to lose the money or let anyone know he had it. They would need every *kreuzer** they had.

---

*Slightly more than one-half cent U.S. money.

There were no barn chores for them to do since their animals were all gone. Their breakfast of hot tea, hard bread, and goat's cheese was soon finished. Uncle Abraham returned thanks at the end of the meal. He asked God's protection and blessing on those who were leaving as well as they who were staying. Following their family custom of singing a hymn together before beginning the day's work, his full, rich voice led out:

O Gott, thun mich erhalten,	(O God do thou sustain me
In miner trawerikeit	In grief and sore duress;
Den hochmut thu zerspalten	Pride counter which distains Thee,
Trost mich in minem leid....	And comfort my distress....)

Christian added his voice to the family chorus as they sang through the eight verses of the familar hymn, asking God to bless and protect them as He had Abraham in his journey to Canaan. Mother's voice failed and tears glimmered on her eyelashes at the words of the last verse:

Gott bin ich dir ergaben	(To Thee my trust I'm giving;
Du wirst min halfer sein	Thou wilt my helper be.
Dir sei hiemit befohlen	Soul, body, child, companion—
Mein seel, lib, kind und weib....	Herewith commit I thee....)

There was a moment of silence after the "Amen" died away. Mother brushed away a lingering tear. She sighed shakily before saying with forced cheerfulness, "Yah well. We may as well be going."

Good-bys were said without any great display of emotion. The German reserve which held their emotions in check did not mean their affections were any less sincerely or strongly felt. An open display of emotion was simply embarrassing.

The heavy trunk was dragged and pushed into the wagon. Mother had packed a bundle for each person to carry which contained their own person-

al things, a change of clothing, and some food. Christian swung his bundle over the side of the wagon and climbed in after it. He squeezed in between his sisters, Anna and Elizabeth. Uncle Abraham cracked the whip over the heads of the oxen, and the wagon wheels began to turn. They were on the way!

Christian waved to his aunt and cousins standing by the gate. He did not know if he was going to laugh or cry. The eagerness to see new things was shadowed by the sadness of seeing the dear old home growing smaller and smaller behind them. It did not know they were leaving and never coming back. Christian watched it as they rode through the streets of Gerolsheim for the last time until it was swallowed up in the gray morning light.

The air was so chilly it did not seem like the middle of April. Christian put his hands under his legs to keep them warm. They were passing the little cemetery now where Father and Grandfather were buried. Warm memories flooded into Christian's heart. He pulled one hand from under his leg and drew his sleeve across his eyes. Straightning up, he saw Peter doing the same thing. At that moment Christian would have been ready to turn back and stay in Gerolsheim.

Anna squeezed Christian's hand comfortingly and said in a husky voice, "We are doing what Father thought best, Christli. It's what he wanted."

A great weight lifted from Christian's heart. Of course! Staying in Gerolsheim would never be the same anyway with Father gone. If going to Pennsylvania was what Father had wanted, he would go and be glad to do it.

Uncle Abraham stopped at the Frey family home

long enough for Jacob Frey's wagon to fall in place behind the Burkholder's. Then the oxen plodded slowly and deliberately the seven miles to Worms, pulling the wagons behind them. The day grew light and warm. Christian ate from his bundle at noon. All the little jiggles and jolts of the wagon grew tiring. His legs were not used to being still so long. They grew cramped and stiff. For a while he and Martin Frey walked behind the wagons. But the discomfort of the long ride was soon forgotten as the town of Worms came near. Soon the real journey would begin!

Uncle Abraham helped Mother secure passage to Rotterdam on one of the Rhine boats and helped them get their trunk aboard. Mother thanked him for his help.

Lifting his hand in farewell, Uncle Abraham blessed the little group by repeating the words of the often-used benediction from Numbers 6:24-26: "The Lord bless thee, and keep thee: The Lord make his face shine upon thee, and be gracious unto thee: The Lord lift up his countenance upon thee, and give thee peace."

"Thank you," Mother said simply as she shook Uncle Abraham's hand in farewell, "and God bless you. Good-by."

Uncle Abraham shook hands with everyone. Then he turned and left the boat. He took his place again on the wagon seat and headed back to Gerolsheim. Once, they saw him turn and lift his hand in a final farewell. Christian raised his hand in return as he stood with his family at the deck railing, watching their last link with home growing fainter in the distance.

Chapter 8

Adventures on the Rhine

The ship which the Burkholder and Frey families had boarded turned into the middle of the Rhine River and headed downstream. The Rhine had always been an important and unusual river. It was important because it was the main highway for anyone traveling a distance. It was unusual because it flowed north from its source in Switzerland, through Germany and into Holland where it emptied into the North Sea.

The river was deep and large enough to accommodate many boats. It was a common sight to see ships going up and down the Rhine. But it was not a common experience for Christian to be on one of the ships. The strange, bouncy feeling of the ship lying low on the watery surface sent quivers up his legs and into his back. He walked unsteadily around the deck with Peter, Hans, and Martin Frey. He slid his hand along the railing to steady himself. He wanted to see everything he could.

Before the ship had gone very far, it stopped at a toll gate below a castle on a cliff high above. If anyone had expected the trip down the Rhine to be made swiftly, they were in for a surprise, Christian learned. From Heilbonn, a little below Worms, to Rotterdam in Holland, there were thirty-six toll gates or custom houses. At each one the ship must be inspected and taxes paid to be able to use that part of the river and continue on. The custom-house officials inspected the ship whenever it suited them. Often the ship was kept waiting several days. The Swissers soon became accustomed to these sometimes long and annoying delays. May 7, Peter's eleventh birthday, passed while they waited at one of these custom houses.

Mother had no love for idleness at home and she intended to keep busy here as well. She and the girls took up needlework and knitting. Ulrich assumed the position of schoolmaster for the younger boys. Peter and Hans Frey learned to do sums and recite long passages by memory under Ulrich's tutoring. Christian and Martin learned to write their names and began to read, using their only two books, the Bible and the *Ausbund,* for textbooks.

Between stops, Christian preferred to spend his days on deck watching the country slide by rather than staying below in the dark and dingy sleeping quarters assigned to their group. He knew he would never forget the beautiful scenery of the Rhine River Gorge. High cliffs crowned by castles towered above on both sides. A crazy quiltwork of vineyards patterned every terraced slope where peasants had been able to gain a foothold. They scrambled from one terrace to another to cultivate the vines.

41

Where the cliffs tapered off to the level of the river, little villages had been built.

When the boat stopped at villages where the Burkholders knew other Swissers lived, they took the opportunity to visit. Their hosts were happy to share meals with them. How good it felt to be full of good, hot food again after so many cold meals on the ship! At one home they were served *himmel und erde*. This mixture of applesauce and potatoes whipped together was a new food to Christian.

If there were no Swisser friends in the village where they had stopped, Mother, Barbara, Anna, and Ulrich took turns staying with their trunk to guard it while the others went into the village to buy fresh bread. It was a welcome addition to the dried foods they had brought from home. Sometimes Christian was also left behind, but usually he went along.

In Mainz they saw the print shop where Johannes Gutenburg had first printed Bibles and books on a new kind of press which made them more plentiful and easier to buy. Further on, at Cologne, they walked by the great cathedral whose twin spires they had seen many miles before they came to the city. The building had been begun 500 years earlier and it still was not finished. Though the huge cathedral was magnificent, none of the Swissers wanted to go inside. It was the throne and symbol of power of the great Archbishop of Cologne. The way this Roman Catholic archbishop had caused the persecution and death of so many Anabaptists was not easily forgotten.

At most of the towns, passengers either boarded or left the ship. Some of them, like the Burkholders

43

and Freys, were on their way to Pennsylvania. Others were going only to another part of Germany or into Holland. Even though the passengers were nearly all Germans, the Swissers were left pretty much to themselves. They were looked on with scorn because of their different beliefs and dress.

While the Swissers wanted to go to Pennsylvania for religious freedom, many of the other Germans wanted to go simply because they hoped to buy land cheaply and become wealthy there. These people often had low morals and could not be trusted.

At many places the Rhine was smooth and broad. But at others, jutting rocks and sharp bends made it dangerous. Christian pricked up his ears when he heard the crewmen speaking of the *Lorelei* as they neared St. Goar.

"The river here is narrow and deep," Ulrich explained the famous legend when Christian asked him what the Lorelei was. "The current is swift and there are dangerous rocks. They say there is a maiden with hair that glistens like gold who sits on a rock above the water. When ships enter this dangerous bend in the river, she sings and combs her long hair. This attracts the attention of the sailors and they forget to guide the ships. They say she has caused many shipwrecks on the river here."

Christian did not really believe such a tale, and Ulrich assured him it was only a story. Still, they all breathed easier when they rounded the dangerous bend in the river and sailed into the wide Mosel Valley beyond.

At Duisburg, the last large town in northern Germany, Christian went with the others to buy food. Their supply from home was almost gone by

44

now. Only Ulrich stayed behind this time. Like most other towns in Germany, the marketplace with an elaborate fountain was the center of the town's activity. Facing the marketplace in the square, were the Town Hall, inns, and shops. Mother bought dark pumpernickle bread, gouda cheese, sausages, and grape juice to take back to the ship.

As the Burkholders started back through the narrow, cobblestone streets leading away from the square, Mother kept throwing hurried glances behind them. Some places the streets were darkened by the upper stories of the half-timbered houses which stuck out over the street like a ceiling. Mother passed through these places so fast Christian had to run to keep up.

"Not so fast," he panted.

"Don't look now, but a man is following us," Mother said in a low voice. "We must get back to the ship as fast as we can. Stay together."

The little group felt relieved as they walked up the gangplank to the ship. Mother glanced back and saw the man follow them on board.

"Let's go down to the others right away," Mother said in an urgent tone.

Christian followed without hesitation. Mother told Ulrich and the Frey family about the man who had followed them.

"I saw that man following us while we shopped," Mother said. "I don't trust him."

Jacob Frey agreed. "You girls stay away from him," he advised. "Don't go anywhere alone. Boys, be sure he doesn't find out you have some money. I'm not sure why he followed you, but if he is

45

traveling on this ship, we had better stay out of his way."

"I hope he soon gets off again," Mother said.

The new passenger was not as easily avoided as they had hoped. He introduced himself as Johannes Wiesher. He said he was a guide for travelers going to Pennsylvania. The Swissers were sure he was what was known as a "newlander." Many of these men traveled through Germany telling fantastic stories about the new land and urging people to go. For a price, a newlander promised to guide people to Rotterdam and arrange passage on a ship going to Pennsylvania. The ship's captain paid the new-lander for every passenger he brought on the ship.

When Mr. Wiesher had seen the Swisser family in Duisburg, it had not been hard for him to guess they were on the way to Pennsylvania. Since there was no father with them, he supposed Mother would easily be convinced to become one of his customers. Time after time he urged her to accept his offer of help. He was a smooth talker and had tricked many a less cautious person into paying a high price for his services, which were of no real value and very little help in the end. His concern was, after all, not for the safety and comfort of his customers, but for the size of his own purse.

Jacob Frey scoffed at Mr. Wiesher's tales of the grief which would come to them when they arrived in Rotterdam without the benefit of his aid.

"We have friends who will help us," Mother insisted.

With a disgusted snort, Mr. Wiesher walked away.

After four weeks of travel, the ship that carried

46

the Swissers at last crossed into Holland. The difference was noticeable almost immediately, not only because of the orange flag that fluttered in the breeze, but the language, customs, and even the food were different. The Dutch spoken here was not the same as the *Deutsch* dialect of German which Christian spoke. The people were wealthier than were the Germans. The land was flat and marshy. The towns were laced with canals and bordered by dikes. Windmills dotted the landscape, their huge wings of fabric tautly stretched over wooden frames.

Several more stops were made for inspections and payment of taxes. The first of June, 1754, was a day Christian never forgot. On this day, his eighth birthday, the ship which had carried them all the way from Worms, docked at Rotterdam.

In the confusion of coming into port and beginning to unload the ship, Peter, Christian, and Elizabeth were left alone. There were so many things to be seen in this bustling port. Ships from all over the world came and went in this harbor. The three Burkholders watched all the activity with wondering eyes.

Suddenly, a rough hand grabbed Elizabeth's shoulder and pulled her back toward a narrow passageway. Terrified, she looked up into the mean, glittering eyes of Mr. Wiesher. He clapped his huge hand over her mouth. The whole world seemed to reel and move in slow motion. Elizabeth heard Peter and Christian yelling, but it seemed faint and far away. Then, the pounding of feet came nearer.

"What do you think you are doing?" Ulrich's familiar voice rang out. "Let her go," he com-

47

manded in his blunt, outspoken way.

As suddenly as she had been grabbed, Elizabeth was released. She staggered backwards and would have fallen if Ulrich had not caught her. Mr. Wiesher was gone.

The whole thing had happened so fast it almost seemed to Peter and Christian it had never happened at all. But Elizabeth knew it had been real. She was badly frightened.

"Oh! What was he going to do?" she screamed in a whisper.

"Maybe he thought you had some money and was going to try to take it. I was just coming around the corner when I saw Peter and Christli pointing and yelling. If it had not been for that, or if I had come a minute later, I don't know what might have happened. But come. We are ready to leave the ship. We will probably never see Mr. Wiesher again," Ulrich comforted her.

"Thank the Lord you got there when you did," Mother breathed when Ulrich told her of Elizabeth's scare. "God has protected us and brought us this far. I know He will be with us the rest of the way."

"Mother, do you need my money?" Christian whispered in his mother's ear.

Mother shook her head and tried to smile. But Christian sensed she was worried. Her smile was not natural. He knew much of the family's money was gone, though the little bag he wore inside his clothing was still heavy.

"We will need it soon enough, Christli," Mother said. "Now come. The Freys are waiting. We must go find Dirk Peters."

48

Chapter 9

Rotterdam

It was not too difficult to find an agreeable Dutchman to take their trunks to the home of Dirk Peters. More of their fast-disappearing supply of money was needed to pay for the hauling, but it could not be helped. The trunks, which must be taken with them, were much too large and heavy to be carried. But to save money it was decided only Ulrich would ride with the trunks and the rest of them would follow on foot. It was a pleasant June day and with so many new and different things to be seen along the way, no one minded having to walk.

The wagon led them through the streets of Rotterdam toward the farmland beyond. They passed bustling street markets where mounds of fresh produce, fish, and cheeses were sold. Christian did not know when he had ever seen so much food at once—especially fish. Street vendors sold herring which customers ate on the spot. Christian stared in disbelief the first time he saw a Dutchman stop and buy a herring. The fishmonger scaled and gutted the whole fish and divided it in half with a quick flick of his knife. The buyer held up the fish by the tail, dipped it in raw onion and swallowed it in two mouthfuls. Later Christian learned the fish was not raw as he had first thought. It had been cured before it was sold. Still, it startled anyone who had never seen it before.

The Swissers walked across high, arched bridges which crossed tree-lined canals. Near the market square they saw shops which sold the famous blue *Delft* porcelain ware. Though the Dutch people all were busy and working hard, no one seemed to be hurried or worried. Everyone went calmly and deliberately about his business. Adding to the peaceful atmosphere was the music of the barrel organ grinders. These huge, magnificently deco-rated organs of carved white wood played waltzes, Dutch clog dances, and a host of other tunes. Christian and the other boys stopped at the edge of a group of children clustered around one of these organs. They watched the organ grinder's muscles bulge and strain as he wound the huge organ. As the tune began to tinkle, the children laughed and began to dance.

"Come along, boys," Mother urged. "We must not let the wagon get out of our sight."

The boys took their places again in the little band. The cobblestone streets of town soon gave way to the country dirt roads. The sounds and smells of Rotterdam faded behind them. Now flat land stretched out to touch the horizon far away. Lush meadows filled with wildflowers and studded with cattle were a welcome sight to these country-born farmers who had seen nothing but towns and ships for six weeks. Far ahead of them the faint speck of the wagon with their trunks turned to the left.

"We will have to walk faster," Jacob Frey urged. "The sun is getting low. We must get there before dark."

They all quickened their pace for a while, but they soon slowed again. They had already walked several miles and were not used to so much exercise after the weeks of inactivity on the Rhine. No one was sorry when Dirk Peters came back in his wagon with Ulrich to meet them and give them a ride to his home.

"I'm glad to see you made it safely. But I am sorry to hear about your husband's death, Elizabeth," Mr. Peters said to Mother in a warm, sincere tone. "A friend of Johannes Deknatal told me just a few weeks ago. You are brave to make the trip alone."

"I promised Christian we would go," Mother replied, her eyes misty with remembrance. "He said God would go with us, and He has. We are thankful for His faithfulness."

Plump, friendly Mrs. Peters made them all feel as comfortable as possible and very welcome in her shining, spacious home. She also offered her sympathy to Mother and the children. Then she set about filling their stomachs and making up beds for them.

Several weeks went by while the family waited for their ship to sail. Mr. Peters took Mother and Jacob Frey back to Rotterdam several days after their arrival to arrange passage on a ship. With his help, they made an agreement with Captain John Spurrier of the ship *Phoenix* for the group's passage.

"There are seven of you," Captain Spurrier said to Mother. "Only one is under ten years of age. He can go half-fare. Six full fares at $19.60 each and one half-fare at $9.80 will be $127.40."

"That is several years' wages. I don't have nearly that much money," Mother gasped.

The captain was firm. "Others without money are going as indentured servants. You could do that," he suggested. "When you arrive at Philadelphia someone will pay your passage for you. In return, you can work for him until it is paid. I can give you the name of someone who might be willing to do that for you."

"We have friends who have promised to help us," Mother said, showing him Daniel Groff's letter.

"All right. You can go as free-willers," Captain Spurrier replied. "The sailing date will be announced when it is known."

While they waited, the women and girls helped Mrs. Peters with all the extra housework they were making for her. Mother and Mrs. Frey also washed and mended all the clothes. They wanted everything clean and tidy before starting the long sea voyage. Mr. Frey and the boys helped Mr. Peters with the farm work. It felt good to be working in the wide, open spaces and fresh, clean air again.

After weeks of scanty meals to save money, Mrs. Peters' hearty, plentiful meals were a luxury. Christian learned to like the tender, tangy herring of Holland as well as potatoes and kale and smoked sausage. A favorite and specialty of the Peters' was a thick pea soup called *snert*. It was a mixture of pork, sausage, and vegetables which was simmered all night. It was delicious!

Several times Captain Spurrier announced a

sailing date. But bad weather or other problems forced the date to be postponed. Although the Swissers were enjoying the fellowship and hospitality of their Mennonite friends, they were eager to continue on. The Peters' home was almost too grand for them to really feel at home. Rotterdam was too worldly and commercial to make them want to stay there. They were eager to finish the journey they had begun. Yet, they knew the next part of the trip was the most dangerous.

A new sailing date was set for the end of June. When it was not again postponed, the two heavy trunks were loaded into Mr. Peters' wagon to take them back to Rotterdam. Mrs. Peters packed a large bundle of herring, sausages, bread, and gouda cheese for each family. Mother was grateful. She had spent the last of the family's money from Christian's little sack to buy some food, but she knew it would never be enough.

"Here is a little something to help you on the way," kind Mr. Peters said, handing Mother some money.

"Ach no! We owe you for all your kindness," Mother protested. "We can't take money from you."

"Do you think I would let a widow pay me?" Mr. Peters asked. "This money is from the church here. Our Mennonite Charity and Emigration Committee gives help to all our needy brethren who are going to Pennsylvania. Please accept this money as a gift of love from the Mennonite church in Holland."

"Thank you," Mother murmured. "Oh, thank you! God is still providing for us."

As they drove through Rotterdam, Christian saw the slums where other German immigrants stayed while waiting for their ships to sail. How thankful he was for their kind friends! Thanks to them, the time spent in Holland had been as refreshing as a cold drink of water on a hot summer day.

When the trunks were safely on board with them, Mr. Peters said good-by and wished them Godspeed. Each of the Burkholders and Freys thanked Mr. Peters again for his kindness as he turned to leave the ship.

There were no regulations as to how much a ship could safely hold. As much cargo as could be carried on board was loaded and as many people as could be crowded on were accepted. All the passengers had to agree to pay the full passage for any of their family members who died at sea after the voyage was half completed. If a person died before the halfway mark was reached, there would be no charge. Mother shuddered, but agreed. There was no other way.

At last the orders were given and the *Phoenix* sailed away from Rotterdam toward the North Sea. If the winds were favorable, they could hope to reach Cowes, England in seven days. That would be their last stop before Philadelphia.

Christian stood at the ship's railing between Mother and Anna, watching as the last sight of the European continent slipped below the horizon.

"No man having put his hand to the plow . . ." Mother said quietly to herself.

Christian looked up, wondering what she meant by that. He saw her square her shoulders and turn to face the open water ahead of them.

Chapter 10

Three Weeks to Cowes

The *Phoenix,* which had looked so big at Rotterdam, seemed to have shrunk. The 576 passengers and cargo were nearly twice the 400 tons the ship was built to comfortably carry. This was Captain Spurrier's third trip across the Atlantic to Philadelphia. He well knew the dangers of the ocean and the hardships passengers would have to endure because of the crowded conditions. But he was not concerned with their comfort. They wanted to go to Philadelphia and if he did not take them, someone else would. He figured he had as much right to make money as anyone else. And if he was going anyway, he might as well make it worth his while. More passengers meant more money.

The *Phoenix* was about 170 feet long and made completely of wood. A few cannons were mounted on her for self defense in the event of meeting pirate ships. But she was not nearly as heavily armed as a warship. Three masts pointed toward the sky. The main mast in the center was the tallest. The sails on these masts and the wind that filled them were the ship's only source of power.

There were four main floors, or sections, on the *Phoenix*. The bottom one was called the mainhold. Cargo such as barrels of food, tools, implements, and other things being exported to Philadelphia were stored there. The two middle floors were called "between decks." All the passengers were crowded into this space. It was filled with bunks which were no more than a narrow shelf, barely two feet wide and six feet long. Under each bunk was a small drawer with a white porcelain knob.

Steep, narrow ladders led from one floor to another. Getting trunks up or down was not easy. The passengers kept their trunks near their bunks rather than storing them in the cargo section. They might want to use some of the things in them during the ocean voyage. And if they wanted to have their possessions when they arrived, it was best to keep the trunks where they could guard them from dishonest passengers.

The top floor was the main deck where the ship's crew members had their quarters and did their work such as cooking in the galley and steering the tiller. The sheep, pigs, and poultry that had been taken on board were kept here.

In the center of the ship was the upper deck. It was open to the weather. Here three lifeboats were nested, one inside the other, with their bottoms up. A railing was built above the high sides of this floor to offer a measure of support and safety to anyone who had business there. Both the bow (front) and stern (back) of the ship were built up a little higher

than the upper deck. The back section contained the Great Cabin which was where the captain lived and the ship's officers ate.

The tops of these bow and stern sections were also open to the weather and had railings on both sides. The bowsprit looked almost like a mast. It wore a flag, but no sails. Rigging for some of the other sails was fastened to it. It stuck out from the bow of the ship like a finger, slicing the air and pointing the way.

Although most of the passengers on the *Phoenix* were Germans, only about forty of them were Swissers, counting women and children. They were nearly all strangers to each other when the ship left Rotterdam. But it did not take long to get acquainted. Their faith and hope of freedom in Pennsylvania were a common bond that drew them together. They wanted bunks as near together as possible. That was not too hard to accomplish since the other passengers did not care to associate with them very much anyway.

Getting to Cowes took much longer than everyone hoped, although it was not unusual for this part of the trip to take even more than the three weeks it took the *Phoenix*. Sailing vessels were entirely dependent on the winds. If a strong wind blew the right direction, the trip was short. If the winds were light, as they were this time, sailing was slow.

Some days Christian thought they could not have moved at all. All around them as far as anyone could see there was only water and more water. They seemed to be glued in the exact middle of a round, blue platter with a high, domed glass cover above them. The ship rocked gently on the little swells that slapped feebly against her sides at the water level. Mother said they could be glad there wasn't a storm, but Christian longed for action. He wanted to be going places and doing things. This slow ride had soon become monotonous. The tightly-packed ship grew swelteringly hot in the July sun. It was not much cooler on deck, but at least the air was fresh. Christian and Martin were not allowed to go on deck unless someone older was with them. And so, much of their time was spent near their bunks in the sticky heat, studying the lessons Ulrich continued to set for them.

Everyone was relieved when near the end of the third week the Isle of Wight was sighted. This island port in the English Channel off the coast of England was a common refueling stop for immigrant ships. The winding streets of Cowes were bordered by picturesque rock and thatch houses. Their steep, gabled roofs sported many chimneys. Blooming roses spilled over low stone walls between the houses. The whole island with its real grass, trees, houses, and just plain, damp earth was a feast for the eyes of these sea-weary travellers who had been cooped up in one small ship for three weeks.

The *Phoenix* rode at anchor in Cowes for another slow two weeks. Inspections were again made and taxes paid. More food and barrels of water were taken on board in preparation for the long sea voyage.

There were no Mennonite friends in Cowes to befriend them. Mother was so thankful for the money from the Mennonite Charity and Emigration Committee. There was enough to pay the custom duties and taxes and to buy some food for themselves. Food here was more expensive than it had been at home, but there was nothing to do except buy it. They needed to eat while they waited and Mother wanted to take at least a six weeks' supply of food with them. The money was going fast.

"I hope we don't stay here much longer," Mother worried aloud. "This sitting here and going nowhere is getting expensive."

"I heard talk that we may leave the day after tomorrow," Barbara reported.

"I certainly hope so," Mother sighed. "But I can't understand why the captain keeps taking on more passengers. This ship was full when we got here. We can't possibly take on any more. I doubt if it is safe already. But we have no choice now. We must go with it, safe or not."

Chapter 11

Perils at Sea

The *Phoenix* slowly turned and slipped out of Cowes. The big moment had arrived at last! It was exciting in a way, and yet sobering. The lives of the 688 passengers were now at the mercy of the captain and the weather. Some, who had been persuaded by newlanders to make the trip, were already homesick. But they had no money to return to Germany, either. They had been forced to commit themselves to being indentured servants. When and if they ever arrived in Philadelphia, their future did not look very bright. They would have to work for their master as much as five to seven years to pay off their passage. Only then would they be able to find their own homes.

The little group of Swissers on the *Phoenix* also had fears and misgivings. But they had something else the others did not all have—faith in God. Though they did not speak of it aloud, they fully realized they might not all live to reach Philadelphia. Not knowing which of them might die made them sober. Even the small children sensed their parents' tension and were quiet. Yet, they knew God was with them. They could trust Him in life or death. He would never fail them.

While some of the passengers mourned and wept at leaving Cowes, the Swissers gathered for prayer. Johannes Kauffman had been unofficially recognized as their leader and spokesman. He read Psalm 107 and led in prayer, asking the Lord's protection on them in this dangerous sea voyage. The Burkholders and Freys were happy for the fellowship of this larger group of Swissers. They did not feel as alone as they had when going down the Rhine.

The group sang a hymn written by Menno Simons: "My God Where Shall I Wend My Flight?" Christian knew some verses of the hymn by memory. The seed of fear in his heart faded away as he blended his voice with the others to sing the last verse:

Veel lieuer kies ick ongemack
Al met Gods kinderen to lyden
Dan ick van Pharao ontfang sijn schat
Om een cleyne tijt met hem te verbliden
Pharaos rijck is titelic
Christus rijck duert eewelyc
Hi ontfangt sijn kinder seer blydelyck.

(I'd rather choose the sorrow sore,
And suffer as of God the child
Than have from Pharaoh all his store,
To revel in for one brief while
The realm of Pharaoh cannot last,
Christ keeps His kingdom sure and fast;
Around His child His arm He casts.)

Life soon settled into a routine of eating, working, and sleeping. Mother and the girls picked up their knitting again while Ulrich continued the boys' lessons. The children of some of the other Swissers joined their classes. Mother's warm smile and helpful hands soon won many friends for her among the other passengers. She was always ready to lend a hand to a tired mother with a fretful child or to do what she could to make a sick person as comfortable as possible in the crowded conditions.

As the weeks wore on, Mother tried to stretch out the family's own food supply by giving them all smaller portions. Warm food was served only three times a week by the ship's cook. Christian was always hungry. It seemed like years since he had eaten his fill at Mr. and Mrs. Peters' table in Holland.

The drinking water in the barrels on the ship had soon become warm and scummy. Now it was turning black and thick. Before drinking, it was necessary to scoop worms off the top of the water. No one drank more than he had to for fear of getting sick. The broiling August sun added to the heat produced by the closely-packed bodies of the passengers and increased their thirst. Children cried piteously for a drink of fresh water. Older people moaned and wept. Hunger and thirst made them irritable and quarrelsome. Mothers and fathers blamed each other for convincing them to come on this trip. The noise of the weeping, complaining, quarreling passengers wore on night and day. There was never a minute of complete silence.

"Oh God! If only I had a piece of good bread," lamented one whose food supply was gone. "Just a drop of fresh water," begged another. "If only I was at home again, even if I had to lie in my pigpen. That would be far better than this!" wept a homesick traveler.

Mother, who had always kept her house neat and tidy, found the uncleanliness of the ship unbearable. There was no extra water for washing. As soon as the last sight of land was gone, many passengers became seasick. Some vomited for days. The ship's crew would do nothing to clean up the mess and the passengers could not. Rats swarmed everywhere. The stench of the odors and fumes confined in the closed area made Christian's head ache terribly. He couldn't think well enough for much study anymore. Lice soon appeared, along with dysentery, boils, scurvy, and mouth-rot from eating the sharply-salted food and drinking the wormy water. More and more people were becoming sick.

Every morning and evening the group of Swissers gathered to worship God and pray together, asking God to spare their lives. Psalm 107 had become real to them in these weeks since leaving Cowes. They often repeated parts of it by memory. Verse six was their favorite. "Then they cried unto the Lord in their trouble, and he delivered them out of their distresses." It helped a lot to remember God's faithfulness to the Israelites on their way to Canaan. He could be trusted to bring them, too, safely through hunger, thirst, storms, and illness.

The Lorents Mangel family, who were quartered near the Swissers, had a golden-haired daughter, Christina, who was five years old. Her sunny smile and quiet ways made her the favorite of many around her. She was one of the first to become dangerously ill. Already frail, her small body wasted rapidly away with dysentery until she

65

seemed to be no more than a shadow of herself. One morning Christian saw Christina's parents standing by her bunk, sobbing uncontrollably. Death had mercifully ended her suffering, but they could not be comforted. Burial was impossible. They watched helplessly as her body was carried away to be dropped overboard into the sea. To have lost her was bad enough. But to think of her body lying at the bottom of the ocean and perhaps eaten by horrible and unknown sea monsters, was worse.

Christina's death was the first of many to follow. It became an almost daily occurrence. Some people, crazed with hunger, thirst, sorrow, and misery, came near to killing each other. Only those who had a firm faith in God and His perfect will were able to patiently endure the suffering and heartaches they knew.

The Swissers were not entirely spared from the sickness and death all around them. One mother died while giving birth to a son who was born dead. Peter's friend, Hans Frey, died with dysentery. No one had much heart for working or studying. And Mother had a full-time job helping to care for the sick.

New fear surged through the ship when a case of measles was discovered in one of the children. A disease like this meant almost certain death for anyone who got it. There were no medicines or even water which was safe to give to one burning with fever.

Christian and Martin Frey were still fast friends, but lately they had not had the ambition to do much besides talk together. They tried to guess what Philadelphia and their new homes would be like. Once they started dreaming of all the good things they would have to eat. But they soon gave that up because it made them too hungry.

One morning Martin did not feel like getting up. His mother stared with dread at the red dots all over his arms and face. They could mean only one thing—measles!

"When were you and Martin together last?" Mother asked Christian.

"Yesterday. Why?" Christian wondered.

"He has the measles," Mother answered. "You better stay away from him. Peter has had measles already, but you have not."

A numbing fear spread from Christian's chest down to his toes. He knew only too well what getting the measles could mean for Martin and for himself if he should get them.

Chapter 12

Measles

Christian's fear of getting measles was almost forgotten when a terrific storm raged for three days. It began on a Sunday morning several days after Martin had gotten the measles. The wind, which had been blowing steadily, suddenly picked up speed and turned into a gale without warning.

The sails, filled almost to bursting with wind, strained at their rigging. The sailors knew a gale like this could easily tear the sails to shreds. But when they tried to furl up the sails, the wind blew so violently that twelve men were not able to manage it. The second-mate climbed up the main-mast, hoping to help the men below. But it was useless. The wind tore the sail from the hands of the sailors. It flapped loosely in the wind and knocked the second-mate from the main mast to the floor of the deck below. He lay lifeless and unmoving. His body was unceremoniously dumped into the frothing ocean with the next wave that washed overboard.

The sea raged and surged. The waves rolled like high mountains over each other and fell roaring into the ship. The two men who manned the pump to keep the ship from filling with water had to be tied to their posts to keep them from being washed overboard.

The *Phoenix* was tossed helplessly up the crest of one wave and then down into a deep canyon with walls of water towering high above on both sides. The ship slammed into one wall and was thrown back against the other. Then it rode up the crest of the next wave and repeated the process.

There had been storms before, but never anything like this. It was impossible for the passengers to sit or walk in their crammed quarters.

"Just lie on your bunk and try to hang on," Mother called through the noise of the storm and moaning people.

Christian tried to hang on, but even that was impossible. He was tossed first one way and then the other. He was thrown out of his bunk and onto the floor on top of another person. He crawled back into his bunk, only to be thrown out again. After a full day and night of battling the rolling ocean, he had hardly any strength left to fight. Both sick and well were thrown out of their bunks repeatedly and tumbled over each other. By the end of the second day, no one thought they could survive the storm. They were sure the ship would either capsize or sink with all the water that had come aboard.

At last, on the evening of the third day, the wind lessened to a dull roar and slowly subsided. But for another day the seas were so wild and high that it

69

was not possible to cook a meal or do anything about cleaning up the mess the storm had caused.

When the storm had finally worn itself out and given up, the passengers and ship's crew were more dead than alive. The few live animals on the ship were sick and the poultry dead. Many of the passengers who were sick before the storm began were now dead. Those who had been well were sick.

Christian knew Martin had died during the storm. He watched Martin's body being carried away. He had no desire to follow and see it being dropped into the sea. He lay on his bunk, sick in body and heart. Martin, who had been his friend at home and had traveled all this way with him, was gone. There were no other boys his age among the group of Swissers except Peter. But Peter had lost his friend, too. He knew how Christian felt and tried to comfort him. Now, more than ever, they two would stick together.

Nearly a week after the storm, Christian began feeling sick late one afternoon. Mother watched him anxiously. The next morning her worse fears were confirmed. He had broken out with the measles. The epidemic had continued to spread among the children. Every day one or more children had been claimed by the threatening jaws of the sea until only a few were left. Christian was one of the youngest passengers still alive. But now he, too, had the measles. Would the never-satisfied appetite of the sea devour the body of another victim? Mother fervently hoped and prayed not.

For days Christian was too sick to know or care much what was happening around him. He grew delirious with fever. He relived in his mind the horror of the storm they had just come through. At times he lay stiffly on his bunk, gripping it until his knuckles were white to keep from falling off. Then he would sit up, point at the huge waves he thought he saw, and scream weakly. Mother was always there, laying her cool hand on his forehead and speaking soothingly. She lay him back on his bunk again and stroked his hair.

"There now. Just lie still and rest. You'll soon feel better," Mother crooned over and over again until Christian relaxed and fell into a fitful sleep.

Day after long day Mother sat by Christian's bunk. When he was restless, she patiently watched and prayed, pleading with God to spare his life. There was nothing else she could do. Her herbs and teas lay useless in the trunk with no clean water to make them.

"Mother, you must get some rest or you will be ill yourself," Barbara insisted one afternoon. "Anna, Elizabeth, and I will watch Christli. You go lie down."

Mother hesitated. She knew Barbara was right. But she did not know if she could tear herself away from Christian's bunk or if she could sleep if she did.

"Mother, you must rest," Barbara repeated, taking her arm and leading her to her bunk.

Mother allowed herself to be led.

"But you must call me if you see any change at all—one way or the other," Mother choked.

"I will," Barbara promised.

The three sisters anxiously watched the flushed face of their little brother for any sign of change. But there was none. More worn-out than she had known, Mother slept longer than she thought she would. Refreshed by this nap, she took up her post again in the evening.

Early the next morning the crisis came. Christian breathed heavily and unevenly. His body burned with fever, yet shook with chills. Mother fell to her knees beside his bunk and held tightly to his hand.

"Oh God!" Mother wept. "If it be Your will, let my little Christli live. Yet, I have committed him to You." She paused and drew a shuddering breath. "May Your will be done."

Peace flooded Mother's heart as she resigned her will to God's. A line of the hymn they had sung when leaving Cowes came back to her. "Around His child His arm He casts." In that sacred moment, she felt the warm, strong arm of God literally enfolding her and giving her strength.

Christian drew a jerky breath and lay quiet. Mother bent low over him and lay her ear to his chest. A steady throb answered her question. Watching closely, she saw his small chest rise and fall in a steady rhythm. He was not dead; only sleeping naturally for the first time in days.

Mother was more easily convinced now to let the girls watch while she rested that afternoon. Worn-out from lack of rest, and with the greatest strain now past, she found it difficult to stay awake when she again took her post in the evening. Her head nodded and she dozed.

Christian shifted slightly and Mother was instantly awake. She saw his face was not as flushed as it had been.

"Christli, are you awake?" Mother asked quietly.

Christian's eyelids fluttered and opened.

"Mam," he whispered, using his childish name for her for the first time in years. His eyes closed and he fell asleep again.

"He is going to get well! Praise God!" Mother breathed, turning her shimmering eyes upward. She did not see the dirty, rough planks above her head. She saw beyond them into the blue expanse she knew was arched above the sails of the ship where was the One who had granted her heart's desire. Her bowed heart overflowed with thanks and praise to Him who had worked the miracle of healing for her Christli.

Chapter 13

Land

Six weeks had passed since the *Phoenix* left Cowes. Hardly a person was left on the ship who felt completely well. Life became a daily struggle to survive. Christian slowly recovered from the measles, but the disease had left him weak and thin. Mother often gave him all or part of her small portions of food at meal times. She said she was not hungry.

"Will we soon be there?" Christian asked for almost the hundredth time.

"I hope so," Mother answered in a tone that sounded more like a prayer than a wish. "Our own food is gone. The little we can buy from the ship's store is spoiled and so expensive. We have only a few kreuzers left. I don't know how long we can live like this."

Christian suddenly realized how old and tired Mother looked. She was much thinner and her face more lined than it had been last winter. Was it really less than a year since they had all been together at home—with Father? It seemed years and years ago.

Home . . . Gerolsheim . . . Uncle Abraham . . . Christian traveled in his mind back home to his family and friends. He thought of the sunny meadows where he had herded the family goats. How he longed to be back in those meadows with fresh air to breathe, good water to drink, and room to run! He thought he could not stand another minute of this swaying, floating cesspool of a ship. But there was nowhere else to be. He simply had to stay there until he died or reached Philadelphia. And only God knew when that would be.

Christian was more homesick than he had ever been before. He tried in vain to hold back the tears that burned in back of his eyes and made his nose tingle. Not wanting anyone to see him crying, he lay face down on his bunk, hiding his face in the crook of his arm and sobbing quietly.

Slowly he became conscious of a change in the mood of the people around him. He looked up to find clusters of people around each porthole. They stared and exclaimed in excited, yet fearful voices at what they saw. Curiosity overcame homesickness, and Christian wormed his way through the crowd to look for himself. The sight he saw made him suck in his breath sharply.

A ship, much like the *Phoenix,* was near enough to be seen clearly, yet far enough away to be a safe distance. The whole ship was a towering inferno of flames. Black smoke rolled up above the flames. Far away, another ship sailed slowly away. No one had to ask. They all knew it was a pirate ship.

"God is still protecting us," Mother breathed thankfully. "Had we been here a day earlier that could be our ship, robbed and burning. We would be lying at the bottom of the ocean. Thank the Lord we were spared!"

Time passed slowly for the ship full of weak, ill passengers. The Burkholders were all suffering various effects of scurvy and malnutriton. Peter and Elizabeth were both dangerously ill with scurvy. At first they had been tired and depressed. Then their skin became puffy and yellow. Their legs and gums were swollen and they ached all over. Scurvy had caused more deaths at sea than any other disease. No cure was known for it. No one spoke of it aloud, but they all knew Peter and Elizabeth could not live much longer unless they soon came to land.

"Oh Lord, how long?" Mother prayed often.

"Please God, bring us to land," ran like a refrain through Christian's mind all day long.

During the ninth week of sailing, hope spread like a tremor through their hearts when it was rumored the sounding-lead had indicated they were nearing land. The ocean depth grew more shallow every day. Each morning Christian woke up thinking, *is this the day we will see land?*

One glad day, Captain Spurrier announced land had been sighted by the lookout with his spyglass. Everyone was excited and frequently scanned the horizon. But no sign of land appeared. At last, on September 27, the outlines of the land were definitely visible to the naked eye.

A great shout swelled through the ship. Christian went with the group of Swissers as all the

76

passengers crept up from below to the upper deck for their first glimpse of the far-off land they were so eager to see. The sight of the land made the sick and half-dead feel alive again. All over the ship a chorus of voices mixed in weeping, singing, praying, thanking, and praising God. The end of the long, tedious voyage was at last in sight! They could bear their misery a few more days with the hope of a safe landing in the near future.

On September 30 the *Phoenix* reached the first land in Philadelphia and sailed into the Delaware Bay. They were fortunate to be able to sail into the harbor without delay. More often than not, ships had to wait for favorable winds to sail up the river and enter the harbor.

Ship traffic increased on this last 125-mile stretch of the voyage as the broad Delaware River narrowed until it was only two miles wide at Philadelphia. Flags of Holland, Old and New England, Scotland, Ireland, Spain, Portugal, Maryland, New York, Carolina,and the East and West Indies fluttered from the masts of ships coming and going in this busy harbor. They carried spices, sugar, tea, rice, molasses, fine clothes, corn, flour, tobacco, lumber, furs, flax seed, and wild and tame animals. Almost anything that was to be had in the world went in and out at Philadelphia.

Christian feasted his eyes on the alternate flat field and thick forests which spread out on both sides of the river. He breathed so deeply of the fragrant cedar-scented air that his chest hurt. Occasionally houses and outbuildings could be seen nestled in the clearings.

Christian had to pinch himself to be sure he was

awake. The broad, smooth-flowing river with the forests on both sides reminded him so much of parts of the Rhine River he almost thought he was dreaming. He stayed on deck watching the approaching city until darkness hid the land from view and only twinkling lights could be seen.

No one had ever seen a city with so much light after darkness had fallen. Some said it was the light from whale-oil lamps lining the streets. They had been put up three years before. It was another of Benjamin Franklin's ideas. He was quite proud of the street lamps and of Philadelphia for being the first city to have them.

Sleep was nearly impossible that night. When light at last stole across the horizon, a low murmur swept through the ship as the passengers greeted the dawn of the most welcome morning of their lives. It was Tuesday, October 1, 1754.

Chapter 14

Tiresome Arrangements

During the early morning hours, the *Phoenix* had slowly sailed the last few miles up the north-westerly course of the Delaware River. The anchor was cast and one more ship was added to the count of 112 ships docked in the port of Philadelphia. It had taken nine torturously long weeks to make the 3600-mile journey from Cowes to Philadelphia. Over 100 lives had been taken during the passage. Of the 688 who left Cowes, 572 remained.

Philadelphia was both a welcome and awesome sight to the nearly-starved immigrants from the German Palatinate. From the deck of the ship, they literally looked up to the city built on high ground. This city, which welcomed and offered equality and freedom to all races and religions, was to them a symbol of hope for a better life in the New World.

Just how different this New World with its new ways was from the old began to be apparent before the passengers ever set foot on land. No walls or

ramparts surrounded Philadelphia as they did the towns in Europe. It was hard to tell where the city ended and the farms began, so gently were they blended on the landscape of what William Penn called his "greene countrie towne."

Immediately upon landing early that morning, the *Phoenix* was boarded by the mayor of Philadelphia and customs officials. Physical examinations were made of all the passengers. Those who had a fever or other contagious disease were taken to sick houses in the city. Captain Spurrier had to pay the expenses for their care until a doctor declared them free of disease. When they received their certificates of release from two justices, they would have to repay the Captain with either money or their possessions, if they had any. Nursing care was sometimes too little and too late. Immigrants who were taken to sick houses often died there without ever leaving them. In 1754, 253 people who died in these places were buried in the Stranger's Burying Ground outside Philadelphia.

The Swissers on the *Phoenix* were relieved when they passed their physical examinations. The names of the men and boys were signed on Captain Spurrier's List of Foreigners by the clerk and interpreter, Mr. Shoemaker. It was endorsed with a Doctor's Certificate, giving them permission to leave the ship.

When this was done, the men and boys filed by Charles Willing, the mayor, and signed their own names to his document. The clerk wrote the names of those who were either too sick or not educated enough to write for themselves. They signed with an X or + behind their names. The Burkholder boys lined up with the others. Peter and Christian stayed together, but several people came between them and Ulrich.

"First and last name here," Mr. Shoemaker said to Peter, pointing at the line where he was to sign.

Peter picked up the quill pen and hesitated. He had been named Hans Peter in honor of Grandfather Burkholder. But he had never been called anything but Peter. Which name should he write? As he hesitated a wave of dizziness swept over him. His face lost the little color it had and beads of cold sweat popped out on his forehead. He was dimly aware of someone sitting him down on the floor and pushing his head between his knees.

"What is his name?" Mr. Shoemaker asked Christian.

"Hans Peter Burkholder," Christian answered, giving Peter's full name.

Mr. Shoemaker signed "Hance Burghalter" and looked up at Christian.

"Can you write your name?" he asked.

"Yes," Christian nodded. He took up the pen and carefully wrote, "Christian Burckwalder." How thankful he was now for Ulrich's teaching!

Mr. Shoemaker told Christian to wait with Peter until he was able to stand up again. Gradually, color came back into Peter's face as the two boys sat watching the line of men and boys passing by. When Peter felt able, Christian helped him to his feet. Mr. Shoemaker gave Peter the pen. He placed an X between the two names Mr. Shoemaker had written for him.

When the last person had signed this second list, Mr. Shoemaker endorsed it with his signature. Now the men and boys were ready to go to the State House[1] to take the Oath of Allegiance and Abjuration. More than 30,000 Germans had come to Pennsylvania in the last forty years. England and many of the English speaking Pennsylvanians were suspicious of them. Benjamin Franklin disapproved of populating Pennsylvania with what he called "Palatinate boors." England feared the number of German immigrants would soon be so large they could organize a rebellion against her. All German males were required to sign their names, promising they would be loyal to King George II of England, and not take part in any rebellion against him.

The men and boys were taken to shore in a smaller boat. There they were led two-by-two to the State House. Ulrich went with one of the other Swissers, Hans Schwartz. But Peter and Christian stayed together again. How strange it felt to have solid ground beneath them as they walked the five blocks to the State House! They had become so used to walking on a swaying ship they had almost forgotten how to walk on the firm, unmoving ground. Still very weak from illness, the two brothers supported and steadied each other as they plodded along behind their leader.

The 100-foot long State House was the most splendid building Christian had ever seen. It was very new. The English plate[2] sparkled in the nine tall window bays of the building's front. It was very high and had a huge, square stair tower on the outside of the south front. Blue soapstone panels accented the area between the two stories. The

---

[1]Independence Hall
[2]glass

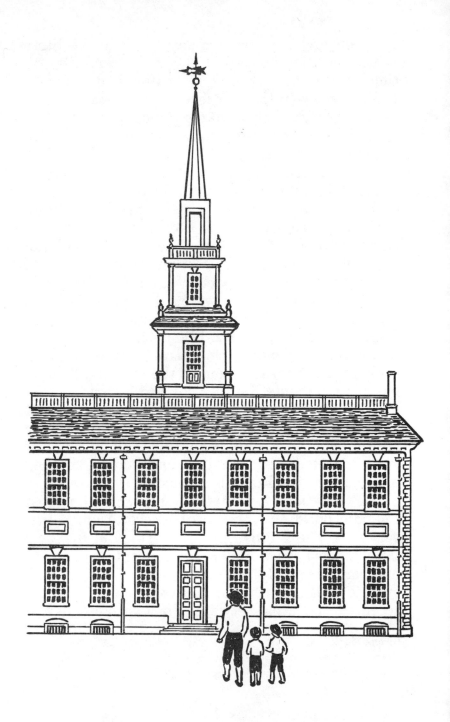

banister along the roof connected the four chimneys at both ends. The building was not joined to any other buildings, but stood by itself.

Christian saw all this as he and Peter followed their guide to the front entrance of the building on Chestnut Street. His legs felt weak and watery beneath him as he stepped inside. The interior of the noble building was so rich and grand he stared in amazement. A row of pillars on each side of a broad aisle formed a framework of arches and supported the floor of the large room overhead.

The two boys glanced through the broad opening of the room on the left side of the center aisle. The Pennsylvania General Assembly was meeting here. Members of the assembly sat at small, green, cloth-covered tables which dotted the room. A large chair and table on a platform in the center of the room was occupied by the leader of the assembly. The clerk was seated just below him to record all the business that was enacted.

"Come this way." The guide led them through the arch into the room on the right which was used for public business.

A long, high desk was the most noticeable feature in the room. It lined the east wall beneath the two windows. Three men were seated behind it. They were conducting a public trial. The man on trial stood in a very small, black, iron cage below the desk. Witnesses sat on short benches to the right of the prisoner.

The immigrants were led to a small table on the left side of the room where they were to sign the oath of allegiance.

"Remember what Mother said," Peter whispered.

Christian nodded. Mother had told them

Swissers obeyed Jesus' command to "swear not at all." She did not want them to swear an oath by kissing the Bible. She had heard the Quaker government of Pennsylvania allowed Swissers to use an affirmation instead of swearing. They should affirm but not swear, Mother had said. Christian wondered how he could explain all this if he were asked to swear.

The mayor, however, did not question the boys. He recognized them as Swissers by the way they were dressed. The clerk merely asked if they could affirm their allegiance to the government. Both boys answered, "Yes." The clerk dipped his feather pen into the inkwell and handed it to Peter. He placed an X between the names "Hans Burghalter," which had been copied for him from the list made on the ship. The clerk dipped the pen into the inkwell again and handed it to Christian. He signed "Christian Burckalder" and returned the pen to the clerk. It was all over in a minute.

"Follow me," the guide said and stepped back into the broad center aisle. They passed the open, spiraling stairway that led to the upstairs library, the office of the Penns who governed the colony of Pennsylvania, and also the long, narrow convention room. The nine tall windows of this second floor room looked out onto Chestnut Street.

Their steps echoed dully on the bare wooden floor as they passed through a narrow passage and out the back door into the State House Yard.* Christian poked Peter. The two boys exchanged grins and then stared at a group of Indians, complete with blankets and feathers, which were camped on the

---

*Independence Square

86

State House Yard. They were a colorful contrast to the depressing appearance of the Walnut Street jail behind them. Christian had never dreamed he would see Indians so soon after he arrived! The guide noticed their interest.

"Those pesky Indians are here to argue about treaties again," he said in broken, but understandable German. "We used to let them stay in the upstairs of the State House. But we had a lot of trouble with them building fires right on the floor. So now they camp outside when they come to talk with us."

When Lorentz Enders and Bartholomeus Beringer, the last of the 316 men and boys, returned to the boat after signing the list, the group was rowed back to the ship. All the legal requirements had now been met. As soon as any passengers paid Captain Spurrier, he was free to leave the ship. A few of the most wealthy passengers were fortunate enough to be able to pay and leave. But most of the passengers had very little or nothing left. They had spent all their money long ago. Their only hope was to sell their services to anyone who would pay their fare for them.

Now a cry unlike any they had heard before swept over the ship. Men looking for cheap labor boarded the ship and began taking away those who had come as indentured servants or redemptioners. Only now did these poor people realize what they had committed themselves to. The buyers were not interested in buying whole families on this white slave market. They wanted the most years of labor they could get for their money. The healthy adults and children went first. Husbands and wives were separated from each other and their children as they were sold to different buyers. Many would never see each other again. To have survived the long, dangerous journey, only to be torn apart when it was finally over, left a trail of broken hearts all over the ship.

A babble of German, English, Irish, and Dutch languages rose heavenward from the *Phoenix* as the immigrants prayed, wept, pleaded with buyers, and said farewells to each other.

"Here is what I'm looking for," a man's voice suddenly said near Christian's elbow. "I could use a young lad like this. Nothing wrong with him if he was fattened up a little. Are you redemptioners, Madam?" he asked Mother in poor German.

"No. Oh, no!" Mother gasped quickly. "We have with us the letter of a friend from Lancaster County. He promised to help us. We will wait for him."

"Too bad," the man muttered as he turned away. "That boy looked like he would make a good, strong worker some day."

A new fear spread through Christian's heart. He knew Mother had no money to pay the family's passage. A healthy young boy brought a high price because he would serve his master until he was 21 and not only the five to seven years a grown man was required to serve. What if Daniel Groff could not come as he had promised? How would he know they were in Philadelphia? Would he have to be sold away from his family?

Christian looked anxiously at Mother sitting among the little group of Swissers. Her head was bowed and her lips were moving silent. He knew she was praying. He bowed his head and began praying too.

Chapter 15

Off the Ship at Last

"Hello! How are you?" a new, friendly voice asked in their own familiar *Deutsch* tongue.

The Swissers looked up first with surprise and then joy. A stocky Swisser man set down a basket of apples. He went around the group shaking hands first with the parents and then with the children, asking their names.

"We are the Christian Burkholder family from Gerolsheim," Mother said when the man reached them.

"I am Ernst Rittenhouse," the man introduced himself. "I am from Germantown. Here, have some apples."

Christian had not been able to keep his eyes off those bright red apples from the moment he had seen them. But he knew it was useless to even think of eating one. They had not one kreuzer left. He swallowed hard and looked away.

"No, thank-you. We cannot buy any," Mother

refused.

"You don't understand," Mr. Rittenhouse said, beginning to hand out the apples. "I didn't bring them to sell. They are free. It's my way of saying 'Welcome to Pennsylvania.'"

Christian gratefully bit into his apple. He thought it was the most delicious thing he had ever eaten. He slowly chewed every tangy, crisp bite to make it last as long as he could.

"Are you looking for Daniel Groff?" Mr. Rittenhouse more stated than asked, looking at Mother and Jacob Frey.

"Yes," Mother and Jacob answered together, wonder and hope mixed in their eyes.

"I have a letter from him promising to help pay our passage. We can't leave the ship until he comes for us. Do you know how we could let him know we are here?" Mother asked.

"He will come for you in a few weeks when he sees your names in Christopher Sauer's newspaper, *Die Pensylvanische Berichte,*"* Mr. Rittenhouse said.

Christian's heart sank. Must they stay on this stinking ship for several more weeks? He didn't know how he could bear the ship when they were in sight of land.

"Your friend knows I make a habit of meeting the ships and finding out who of our Swisser brethren is on them," Mr. Rittenhouse continued. "He gave me enough money to pay the passage for all of you, if you need it. My wife and I are prepared to keep you at our home until he comes. Now, do you have

---

The Pennsylvania Report

any money for your fare? How much do you need?"

Jacob Frey had enough to pay his wife's and his own passage. But he needed help for their daughters. He was also being charged for the passage of his two sons who had died on the way, since they had lived past the halfway mark of the trip.

"I'm sorry, but our money is completely gone," Mother admitted. "We haven't one kreuzer to put towards our passage."

"That's all right," Mr. Rittenhouse assured her. "Daniel Groff gave me more than enough, I'm sure, to cover your needs."

The Burkholders and Freys gratefully stood by watching as Ernst Rittenhouse paid Captain Spurrier the full fare for their families. Their trunks were loaded onto his wagon. They said good-bye to the other Swissers still waiting to leave the ship.

Christian had no regrets at leaving the *Phoenix*. It seemed like he had been in prison for a long time and had at last been released. He felt so light and free he could have shouted for joy as he climbed into their new friend's wagon. Ernst laid Elizabeth gently on a feather tick in the back of the wagon. She was too weak to sit up. Mother sat near her in the wagon bed. Peter refused to lie down. He sat propped against the side of the wagon. He did not want to miss seeing anything.

Mr. Rittenhouse alternated between asking Mother and Jacob about friends and conditions in Germany and pointing out things they were passing in the city. From Market Street, where they were driving, he pointed north up Second Street to the high spire of a church.

"You could not help noticing that steeple from the

91

harbor," Mr. Rittenhouse said. "It is the highest point on the skyline. That is the Christ Church. It was built as part of the agreement between King Charles II and William Penn. The English governors and officials worship there."

Christian got only a glimpse of the brick church as they crossed Second Street. He leaned forward then to hear what Mr. Rittenhouse was saying.

"Ben Franklin has a print shop between Third and Fourth Streets. I'll point it out when we come to it. He gives our printer in Germantown some pretty stiff competition. Christopher Sauer prints mostly German, and Franklin has tried to ruin his business. He started printing a German almanac a few years ago. But too many people liked Sauer's German almanac better and Franklin had to give it up. He does well with his English almanac though. He calls it the *Poor Richard's*. There it is," Mr. Rittenhouse said as he pointed to the open door of 520 Market Street.

Christian heard the thud of the heavy wooden press and saw sheets of paper drying on racks above it before the wagon passed by. Mr. Rittenhouse turned south off Market Street to go down Fourth Street to Chestnut Street.

"I want you to see the State House where your boys were taken to sign," he said to Mother as they approached the grand, impressive State House between Fifth and Sixth Streets. "A bell was shipped from England two years ago when the tower was built. The bell was rung to test it while it was being hung, and it cracked. Pass and Stowe recast it twice in their foundry here in Philadelphia. They finally got it up last year."

The women and girls were as amazed at the beautiful building as the men and boys had been the day before. The bell* clanged the hour as they passed. Who would have thought a country as new as Pennsylvania could have such a fine building as this?

There were many fascinating things to be seen as they rode through the streets of Philadelphia. This city was the capital and largest city of the colonies. There were already 2300 houses in it, and it was growing rapidly. The city was so large it would take almost a day to walk around it. The broad, straight streets were crossed with many smaller alleys and lined with fine, large, four-story stone or brick houses with cedar-shingled roofs and plate glass windows. Many of the houses had two benches set out in front of them. A roof slanted over the benches to make a strange sort of garden pavilion.**

There were brick kilns, tannery yards, sawyer's rigs, blacksmith shops, iron and glass foundries, besides the shops of two printers and many merchants in the bustling, busy town. The odors of fish, salt, and pitch mixed with the smell of the sea and wafted back over the city from the dockside area. The streets were all marked by signs giving their names in both English and German. There were no town clocks to be seen. That seemed odd to Christian. But he supposed one could soon become accustomed to telling the time by listening to the bell, which could be heard all over the city.

People walked on flat stones in spaces between

*Liberty Bell
**porch

93

the houses and streets. About every three feet a high post was set to make a sort of fence between the street and the walkway. These were intended to protect the pedestrians from careless teamsters and dirt thrown up by the horses. Great heaps of garbage and filth rose up above and blocked the gutters. The city was not as attractive as it had been from a distance.

Many plainly-dressed Quakers could be seen walking along the streets. There were also some black house servants. But there were many other men and women dressed according to English fashions. The men's clothes were made of fine English cloth. They wore thin, light coats or jackets of linen or dimity. Many of them wore wigs.

The women wore no hoop skirts, but what they did wear was both neat and costly. Their dresses, which reached down to their silver-buckled shoes, were covered by white aprons. Instead of the European custom of wearing straw hats, some of the women wore fine, white hoods. These were embroidered with flowers and trimmed with lace and streamers. Others wore beautifully-colored bonnets of taffeta. Their hair was frizzed or cut short. Strings of beads circled their necks and costly stones glittered from drops in their ears. Their hands were covered with embroidered and lace-trimmed velvet or silk gloves.

Christian knew already why this was called the New World. It really did seem like a whole new world, so far away and different from Europe. He was glad when Mr. Rittenhouse turned northwest onto Germantown Avenue and the city lay behind them. The ten miles of open country between Phila-

94

delphia and Germantown was much more appealing to him than the busy city.

He began to feel even more at home as soon as they came into Germantown. Here everyone except the Quakers spoke German, and they all were much more simply dressed than the people in Philadelphia had been. The village, with a population of around 3000, stretched out about three miles along Main Street. The growing village was fast becoming a wealthy little town from its manufacture of woolen stockings and its tanneries and mills along the Wissahickon Creek.

Mrs. Rittenhouse came out to the wagon to welcome the newcomers when her husband drove up to the house. She shook hands with them all. Her handclasp was so warm and sincere, Christian felt they were fast friends even though they had just met.

Experience had taught Mrs. Rittenhosue what a new immigrant family wanted and needed most. Even though it was late afternoon, she set out a meal for them of cold meat, bread, butter, cheese, and plenty of drink. The bread was fresh and good, not full of red worms and spider nests as it had been from the ship's store. The water was sparkling clear and good. Christian had not been so full of good food since he left Holland.

After they had eaten, their hostess provided warm water and homemade soap for them to take turns bathing. Mother opened the trunk to get clean clothes for everyone. She found the things around the edges of the trunk had been soaked with sea water and were spoiled.

"It must have happened during the terrible storm just before Christli got the measles," Mother said.

"Well, we still have him, so we won't complain if we lost a few other things."

Mrs. Rittenhouse found some clothes for them to use until they could wash their own. They did not fit exactly, but they covered and they were warm. That was what mattered most.

Elizabeth's needs were taken care of first, since she was the most ill. She was put to bed in one of the good beds downstairs. The long ride in the jolting wagon had quickly worn away her small reserve of strength. She wearily sank into the straw-filled mattress on the rope bed and covered herself with a feather tick. Rest and good food would soon make her well.

Peter washed next and then Christian bathed in his turn and dressed in clean clothes. He had never in all his life been so glad to bathe. At last he was rid of the reeking odor of the filthy ship. He felt like a new person!

Though Mother sent him to bed before dark, Christian made no objection. He was glad to climb the steps to the upstairs where mats were laid out for all the children to sleep in one big, open room. He and Peter lay their mats near the chimney in the center of the room and covered themselves with a feather tick. It would be chilly by morning.

Christian was grateful to be able to stretch out. He was still weak from having measles. The excitement of the day had worn him out. How good it felt to have the solid floor that did not pitch and sway under him! He could even turn over if he wanted to without falling out of bed. Almost as soon as he stretched out, he fell asleep. He was full, clean, and completely comfortable for the first time in months.

Chapter 16

Germantown

Christian slept long and soundly. Only after Peter shook him and tickled the soles of his feet, did he awake.

"Wake up, Sleepyhead," Peter grinned. "We are in Pennsylvania, and it's time for breakfast."

Christian sat up and rubbed the sleep from his eyes.

"Is it morning already?" he asked.

"It has been morning for a long time," Peter laughed. "Mother just came up and told us to come for breakfast. Come on! We're not going to miss the best breakfast we had since we were in Holland."

"Now if there is anything the boys can do to help you, just tell them," Mother said to Ernst Rittenhouse after breakfast.

"I think they could pick up some apples for me," their host decided. "We are making cider just now and there are still a lot of drops under the trees."

The work was not hard and Peter could rest

97

whenever he grew tired. It was a perfectly lovely day. The sapphire sky over the sun-dappled orchard was clear and full of clean, fresh air. Any kind of weather would have suited Christian. He was so happy and full of life he thought he would burst. Before going to his own work, Mr. Rittenhouse told the boys they could eat all the apples they wanted while they worked. Christian intended to eat only one, but that one was so good he ate another and another and another. He thought he would never get tired of the delicious apples even if he ate a whole tree full of them.

The weeks of waiting for Daniel Groff to arrive for them could be well used to gather strength for traveling to their new home, as well as other preparations. Jacob Frey talked with many other immigrants and the men from Germantown to find out where he could buy good land at a price he could afford. Mother and the girls spent many days spinning flax to weave homespun cloth for all the clothes their family required. Mrs. Rittenhouse gave Mother a share of the spun flax in return for their work. Ulrich was busy either helping Mr. Rittenhouse with his work or working with his younger brothers digging potatoes and making cider from the dropped apples. In the evenings he whittled a supply of the wooden bowls and spoons they would need when they settled in their own home.

Making cider was a slow process, but Christian thought it was well worth the effort. The apples were first put into a trough and crushed with a wooden stamper. The mashed mass was put into a basket and hung over a tree branch. It was covered with a clean cloth and weighted down with heavy stones. The clear, brown apple cider dripped through the basket and into a tub set below it. Christian never could decide if he liked the fresh, plain apples best or the nippy cider. It was a fine substitute for grape juice, the common German beverage. So far no one had been able to grow grapes successfully in Pennsylvania, although some were trying. Perhaps someday someone would learn the secret of growing something other than the bitter wild grapes, which were all that grew in this country. Life without grapes would be strange, but not unbearable with the delicious apples and cider to replace them, Christian decided.

Mother wanted to let Uncle Abraham, back in Gerolsheim, know the family had arrived safely in Pennsylvania. She asked Mrs. Rittenhouse how it could be done.

"Write your letter and Ernst will take it to Sauer's print shop when he goes to see if there is any mail for us," Mrs. Rittenhouse said. "He always goes at least every two weeks anyway to get the newspaper."

Mother carefully planned what she wanted to write before she filled the sheet of paper Mrs. Rittenhouse gave her with her small script of closely written lines. She knew Uncle Abraham would be anxious to hear about their trip and the new land. So many of their friends at home had tried to discourage her from setting out on the long trip. She wanted them to know God had protected them and all their lives had been spared.

"Who would like to go along to Sauer's print shop?" Ernst asked one day.

By the way he looked at them, Christian and

Peter knew he was asking them if they wanted to go with him.

"I would! I would!" the boys chimed.

The print shop was a busy, interesting place. It was the center of attraction in Germantown. It was the place to meet and swap stories. Mail to and from Europe went in and out of the shop. Like all printers, the Sauers sold stationery, books, and other odds and ends in addition to printing. They also ordered books from Germany for their customers.

Mother's letter was given to an old man with a long, white beard whom Christian and Peter learned was Christopher Sauer I. He would see the letter got on a ship going to Germany. The kindly old man shook hands with the boys and asked their names. His son, Christopher Sauer II, took care of the printing business. But the elder Sauer had plenty of time to visit and give his opinion on matters which were being discussed by the customers in his shop.

Mr. Rittenhouse was in no hurry to leave after he had picked up his copy of *Die Pensylvanische Berichte*. While he visited and caught up on local news with the other men in the print shop, Christian and Peter looked around. They knew better than poking their noses into things, but their sharp eyes saw everything.

Several workers were setting type by hand, letter by letter and line by line. Two men operated the press. One man did the actual work of printing and running the press. The other kept the press inked. It was hard work and took teamwork to produce perfect printed sheets of paper. When this latest edition of the newspaper was completed, Henry Kepple would carry bundles of them from the print shop to inns and stores in the Tulpehocken and Lancaster, Pennsylvania and Frederick, Maryland areas. From these places the newspapers would find their way to the subscribers.

Die Pensylvanische Berichte looked much like any other newspaper being printed in the colonies. Sauer used very small type and crammed his paper full of world, American, and local news and ads. The paper gave advice on small things such as how to spin and weave wool, or large things such as the evils of war.

Christian's eyes were drawn again and again to a small stack of German Bibles setting on a table along the back wall of the print shop. Later he learned Sauer's Bible was the first one to be printed in the colonies. An unbound copy could be bought for $1.44. For those who did not want to do their own binding, $2.16 would buy a bound copy. The price was far out of his reach now, but in Christian's heart was born the dream of owning his own Bible. He promised himself he would work and study hard until he could own and read his very own Bible.

The first Sunday the Burkholder and Frey families were in Germantown was not a church Sunday. On the Sunday when no services were held, the father of the family was expected to gather the children and teach them how they should live and why. Christian listened respectfully to all Ernst Rittenhouse had to say. But he was glad when they walked to a real service the next Sunday at the Germantown Mennonite Church.

The Germantown meetinghouse was a log building constructed in 1708 after the Old Flemish* pattern. Christian followed Ernst Rittenhouse as he led the Burkholder boys to a backless bench in one of the two men's sections set on either side of and facing the center women's section. Mother and the girls sat with the other women and girls in this center section where the benches faced forward towards a very long pulpit.

The ministers met in a side room to pray and decide who would have the sermons. While they were there, the singing began. Christian closed his eyes and listened to the slow, chanting melody of hymn number thirty in the *Ausbund,* "Herr Gott! Dich Will Ich Loben" (Lord God! To Thee Be Blessing). If he did not see the strange faces and building around him, it was not hard to imagine he was in church in his own home in Gerolsheim. All the hardships of the last half year were forgotten as his full heart overflowed and his voice joined in singing:

Darum so will ich singen,	(Therefore will I be singing
Zu Lob dem Mamen dein,	In blessing of Thy name,
Und ewiglich verkunden	Eternally praise bringing
Die Gnad, die mir erschien.	Of grace that to me came;
Nun bitt ich dich vor all dein Kind,	Before Thy children hence I pray
Wollst uns ewig bewahren	That Thou wilt keep us ever
Vor allen Feinden g'schwind.	From foes without delay.)

When the last of the thirteen verses of the hymn had been sung, the ministers came out to sit behind the preacher's pew (pulpit), with the oldest one leading the way. One of the ministers preached the first of two hour-long sermons. This one was in the Dutch language of Holland. The minister did not

---

*A kind of Mennonites.

speak from a text or open a Bible during his sermon. Christian sat quietly through this sermon although he did not understand much of it. His own thoughts kept his mind busily occupied. When the minister had finished, everyone knelt for a silent prayer with their faces turned toward the backs of their benches. The prayer ended when the oldest minister got up.

Everyone else also stood up and remained standing with their backs to the deacon as he read the morning text from Matthew 6. The words fell like drops of refreshing rain on the hearts of the immigrants in the congregation that morning. "Lay not up for yourselves treasures upon earth. . . . But lay up for yourselves treasures in heaven. . . . Take no thought for your life, what ye shall eat, or what ye shall drink; nor yet for your body, what ye shall put on. . . . Behold the fowls of the air . . . your heavenly Father feedeth them. . . . Consider the lilies of the field . . . even Solomon in all his glory was not arrayed like one of these. . . . Your heavenly Father knoweth that ye have need of all these things. But seek ye first the kingdom of God, and his righteousness; and all these things shall be added unto you." Although they had almost nothing with which to begin their new life, God would provide if they trusted Him.

A second sermon followed the reading of the Scripture. This minister preached in the German Christian could understand and follow. The practice of preaching in both languages during the same service had been developed in order to accommodate the Mennonite settlers of both the highlands (Switzerland and Southern Germany) and

104

the lowlands (Northern Germany and Holland) of Europe. According to tradition, the second sermon began with the Creation in Genesis, went through the Old Testament and ended with the New Testament. When the minister had finished, the other ordained men and some of the oldest men in the congregation gave testimonies. A closing prayer was read from a prayer book, Die Ernsthafte Christen = Pslicht (A Devoted Christian's Duty), while the congregation knelt. When they rose from their knees, they stood with their backs to the minister while he gave the benediction. Two closing hymns were sung, and church was dismissed.

Christian met many new people after the service. He had never seen so many friendly strangers before. They all seemed to know what it felt like to be in a strange place and how to make visitors feel welcome. Even though he had always been used to worshiping in the homes of members of the church instead of a meetinghouse, the pattern of worship was much the same. He could sense a common bond between himself and these people. The faces and places were different, but they all had the same God.

Chapter 17

Riding on a Conestoga Wagon

The Burkholder and Frey families had been in Germantown almost four weeks. One afternoon a Conestoga wagon, pulled by six horses, rattled up to the barn and stopped when the driver called out, "Whoa! Whoa there!"

Christian looked out of the open top half of the barn door in time to see a plainly-dressed, solidly-built man leap to the ground.

"Daniel! How are you?" Ernst Rittenhouse greeted the visitor.

"Pretty good," the man answered. "I hear you have some people here I'm looking for."

"Yes, we do," Ernst said. "And they will be glad to see you."

Christian looked at the man with new interest as Mr. Rittenhouse introduced him to Jacob Frey. This was the Daniel Groff who would take them to Lancaster County! The men exchanged greetings and began discussing Jacob's plans for his family's

future.

"This must be one of the Burkholders," Daniel said as Ulrich rounded a corner of the barn. "At least he looks like a Burkholder."

Ulrich smiled when he heard this familiar statement and came forward to meet the man who had spoken.

"Ulrich, this is Daniel Groff," Ernst introduced the two as they shook hands. "Boys, come out and meet your friend," he called to Christian and Peter, who stood half in and half out of the barn door staring at the beautiful Conestoga wagon and its three double hitches of horses. They had never seen such a sight.

The entirely hand-made wagon was long and deep. It was built with a sag in the middle so if the load inside shifted when traveling over rough and hilly ground, it would slide to the wagon's middle instead of the ends. A white hemp homespun cover stretched over hoops and followed the curves of the wagon body. The front and rear ends of the cover had a high bonnet shape. The top of the front hoop was eleven feet from the ground. The rear wheel was five feet high. The wagon and horses together stretched a distance of sixty feet.

The two boys came shyly out to shake hands with the man who stood beside the impressive wagon. The moment Christian felt the firm, warm handclasp, he knew he had found a sincere friend who could be trusted for a lifetime.

After Ernst had stabled Daniel's horses, they went into the house to meet the women and girls and get something for Daniel to eat.

"I'm glad to see you all arrived safely," Daniel

said to Mother when the introductions had been made. "I got Ulrich's letter with my *Die Pensylvanische Berichte*. I'm sorry Christian did not live to come with you. We could have used him in our church here. But we know God makes no mistakes."

"We miss Christian very much. But we are thankful God has kept us all alive and brought us safely here," Mother said.

"And you are all well?" Daniel asked.

"Elizabeth was quite ill when we arrived. None of us was completely well. But the fresh air and Mrs. Rittenhouse's good cooking has done a lot for us," Mother answered.

"Do you think you are well enough to go home with me?" Daniel asked. "It is a two-day trip."

"We are eager to go and get settled," Mother said. "We are ready to go whenever you say."

"On my way to Philadelphia, I met my old friend, Christian Herr. (His grandfather, Hans Herr, was the first settler in Lancaster County.) We traveled together since we both had loads of wheat to sell. We agreed to start for home together on Tuesday morning. Jacob tells me he has decided to try to find land near York. He can ride with Christian Herr to Pequea, which is further west than we are going. He can find his way from there to York to scout around for land. But his family had best stay here and wait until he has found a place. He can send for them when he is ready."

When Christian awakened on Tuesday morning, he ran to the window to see the day. The sky was clear and the day promised to be fair, though the air was nippy and a thin frost glittered on the ground.

Right after breakfast the men loaded the Burk-holder's trunk into Daniel's wagon. Mrs. Ritten-house packed a large bundle of food for them to eat on the way. Ernst wished them a safe trip and God's blessing, and added a basket of apples to the load.

"Christli must have his apples," Ernst said with a twinkle in his eye. He had seen how much Christian loved apples.

"Thank you so much for all you have done for us," Mother said fervently. "We will never forget your kindness."

"We are here to help each other," Mrs. Ritten-house said. "I am sure you would have done the same for us if things were the other way around."

Christian climbed up after Peter into the covered wagon. Daniel took his place on the seat beside Ulrich, and the wagon lurched forward, following the one in which Christian Herr and Jacob Frey were riding. Christian returned the waves of Mr. and Mrs. Rittenhouse who stood at the gate watch-ing them leave. In a way it seemed like the day they left Gerolsheim. And yet it was different. How long ago that seemed now! They had seen and learned so much in the spring and summer that had passed. Now it was autumn and in just a few days they would at last come to the place they had traveled so long to reach.

Christian's thoughts were interrupted by Daniel's voice, saying, "If we followed the Man-atawny Road* out of Germantown, we would come to Reading and Tulpehocken in Berks County. A lot of Germans have settled there, but not we Swissers.

---

*Route 422

110

To go west to Lancaster County and the Swisser settlement, we will first go south to Philadelphia and then west on the King's High Road. My father, Hans, helped lay out that great road in 1733. It has sure been a big help to us. All we used to have was the narrow Conestoga Road. It was not much better than a trail. A person could travel on horseback, but it was not wide enough to get through with a wagon. We are not nearly as isolated from the rest of Pennsylvania since we have this good road. Lancaster County is being settled much faster since it is so easy to get to and from Philadelphia."

The little wagon train drove to the end of High Street in Philadelphia and was ferried over the Schuylkill River. The hard-packed earth of the King's High Road led the way now through the rolling hills of the district William Penn had given to the Welsh settlers. The names of the towns such as Merion, Bala, Cynwyd, Bryn Mawr, and Berwyn immediately identified them as Welsh in origin.

"William Penn used to worship at the Quaker Meeting House in Merion," Daniel said. "They say one of the reasons he came here was to see Dr. Thomas Wynne. He and Dr. Wynne came together to Pennsylvania on the *Welcome*. The church was built in 1695 and Dr. Wynn built a new house a little beyond it just before 1700."

The road ran tirelessly uphill and down through forests of oak, hickory, and chestnut. For the next 25 miles the elevation increased steadily, but so gradually it was hardly noticeable. Here and there were the clearings of farms and settlements, or the beginnings of them. The day had grown sunny and warm. Christian had two reasons to be glad when a halt was called at noon. His breakfast, plentiful though it had been at the time, had disappeared long ago. And he was glad to stretch his legs, which were cramped from sitting so long.

The multicolored leaves were just past the peak of their beautiful fall colors. They were beginning to drift lazily down to add another layer to the thick carpet of dry, brown, rustling leaves of past generations on the forest floor. The strange shape of a bright yellow leaf captured Christian's attention. It looked exactly like a mitten.

"Look at this funny leaf," Christian said, holding the leaf up by its stem for Peter to see.

"That is a sassafras leaf," Daniel said. "Sometimes the leaves have three fingers, sometimes none, and some are like that. Here, smell this." He broke a small branch from the tree.

Christian sniffed a spicy fragrance unlike anything he had ever smelled. He passed the branch around for his brothers and sisters to smell, too.

"The bark and roots of the sassafrass tree make a tea which is a good medicine," Daniel said. "When we leave the old country we lose some things, but we gain others."

Soon after the wagons again started west, they passed Admiral Warrens Tavern. It was a fairly new one replacing the old Ye Admiral Vernon which had stood nearby. Here the road descended down the southern slope of a mountain into the Chester Valley.

The woods seemed full of wild game. More than once, graceful antlered deer had bounded across the road. Wild turkeys flew up constantly, squawking in protest at the wagons and people who were trespassing on their property. Gray squirrels chattered incessantly as they busily raced up and down trees, hurrying to increase their hoard of nuts before the winter arrived. Their bushy tails waved everywhere like little flags.

"I never saw so many squirrels," Barbara marveled.

"They are a downright nuisance," Daniel said. "Our county government pays a bounty of three pence a head for squirrel scalps. A man can make a better living by shooting squirrels than by day labor. Bounty was paid for 840,000 squirrels several years ago, and they are still a pest to us farmers."

"They are so pretty. It seems a shame to kill them," Barbara said, pitying the little creatures.

"Their looks are better than a rat," Daniel said, "but their manners are not much better. When they get into the shocks, they make a mess in a hurry. Blackbirds are bad pests too. There is a bounty of three cents a dozen for them. And the bounty on a wolf is $2.40. So you can see why it is hard to find a man willing to work in the harvest for 30¢ a day when he can earn more for a day of bounty hunting."

"Are there a lot of wolves in Lancaster County?" Ulrich asked.

"Not as many as squirrels and blackbirds, of course," Daniel answered. "But there are too many for comfort. They make it almost impossible to raise sheep and goats. We have a good many black bears, too. There is plenty of mast, and we could easily raise hogs to sell if it were not for the bears. It seems they are partial to pork."

The horses jogged steadily on through the afternoon. Occasionally they met a wagon piled with sacks of grain or barrels of whiskey, headed toward Philadelphia. Once they passed a big wagon train of 25 wagons which had stopped to repair a broken axle on one of the wagons.

"I hope to reach Downing's Mill by night," Daniel said. "That is the halfway mark to Lancaster. It's the only place between Philadelphia and Lancaster where two buildings stand together. It was first called Milltown because it had the only mill around. I remember my father loading several bushels of wheat on his horse and coming here to trade them for salt. He could get about four bushels of salt for one bushel of wheat. He built a mill as soon as he could, but until then my mother ground our grain with a mortar and pestle."

"How much further is it to Downing's Mill?" Ulrich asked.

"Just a few more miles," Daniel said. "At the Ship's Tavern Inn we can get a good hot meal and a place to sleep. The place does a pretty good business."

"Don't go to that expense for us," Mother protested. "We can sleep in the wagon or on the ground."

"You will do no such thing," Daniel said firmly. "I wouldn't think of letting you sleep out in the night air, especially not when it is so cold at night. We will all stay at the inn. It won't cost too much."

As dusk gathered, Christian watched eagerly for the swinging signboard of the Ship's Tavern. A hot meal sounded good to him at the end of the long day. And he was not disappointed when he got to the table of the inn. There was fried ham, corned beef and cabbage, beef stew, bread made of rye and cornmeal, and tea. Everyone reached across the table, or even across three or four persons, to help themselves to whatever they wished. Each person used the knife from which he ate to carve a slice of meat from the large piece on the platter. If anyone left the table without having eaten enough, it was his own fault.

Christian lay in bed listening to the clinking of dishes in the kitchen below him and the stirrings of the night outside. He did not know what made him think of Martin Frey just then, but suddenly he remembered how he and Martin had so often tried to guess what Pennsylvania was like. They had not guessed the half of it, he knew. And he had only begun to see it.

Just as he was drifting off to sleep, an eerie call floated through the darkness, "Whip-poor-will, whip-poor-will."

Christian sat up and listened as the call came again. Nothing else stirred.

"Ulrich!" Christian whispered urgently through the darkness. "Ulrich, what was that?"

"I don't know," Ulrich admitted. "But we are safe in the inn. Go to sleep."

Christian lay down again. The eerie cry grew fainter. Whatever it was, it was going away. He was glad he was not sleeping in the wagon tonight. But first chance he got he would ask Daniel what the strange sound had been. A wide yawn nearly split Christian's face in two, and he fell asleep wondering what all new and wonderful things he would learn when morning came.

Chapter 18

More New Country

The smells of tea, fried potatoes, ham, mush, and molasses mingled to greet Christian when he awoke in the morning. Daniel Groff insisted on their eating the good, hot meal before they started west. At noon they could eat the rest of the cold things Mrs. Rittenhouse had packed. And by evening they should be home.

Home! Visions of the half-timbered house in Gerolsheim rose up in Christian's memory. They were a long, long way from home. He wondered if this strange country would ever feel like home to him.

The little wagon train crossed the east fork of the Brandywine Creek as they left Downing's Mill and headed west.

"What road is that?" Ulrich asked, pointing to the right where another road joined the King's High Road.

"That is the Paxton Road,"[1] Daniel answered. "It goes to Weber's Thal[2] where many of our Swisser people have settled. Further along on that same road is Ephrata. A group of Donkers is living there since 1735. Most of them vow to stay unmarried and live in a group of common buildings. There are a few families who live in houses around the community. They live by very strict rules, rising for an hour of prayer services at midnight, fasting often, and so on. Their leader is Conrad Bissel. They have a printshop and do very good work. They recently printed the *Martyrs Mirror* in German for our church. They have some odd beliefs, like keeping Saturday as the day of worship instead of Sunday. But in Pennsylvania all are free to worship as they choose, so no one bothers them. Sometimes I wonder if Pennsylvania has too much freedom. All sorts of strange religions might begin here until there is such a mixture that the true faith of Christ is lost. But so far this freedom has been a great blessing to us Swissers.

"We could go home by the Paxton Road," Daniel added. "But it would be the long way around, and the road is not as good as this one."

Christian had been wanting to ask Daniel about the noise he had heard in the night. After a proper length of silence had passed, he could wait no longer.

"Last night there was something outside that went 'Whip-poor-will, whip-poor-will.' What was it?" Christian asked, imitating the sound the best he could.

---

[1]Route 322
[2]Weaverland

"Oh that was a bird," Daniel answered.

"A bird!" Christian exclaimed in surprise.

"Yes. It is a night bird. They live in the woods. You will often hear them at night," Daniel explained. "What did you think it was?"

"I didn't know," Christian confessed. "Ulrich didn't know either."

"I wouldn't expect him to," Daniel said. "It is an American bird. We have some other birds here you didn't have in Europe. We have green woodpeckers with red heads. There is a tiny little bird called a hummingbird. It can fly forward or backward or it can hover in midair. There are also bobwhites. In the spring you can hear them calling their name in the meadows. There is another bird that can imitate all the sounds of the other birds. He makes an awful racket. That's the mockingbird. There are bright red cardinals with a peaked cap on their heads and another bird that's altogether blue. Naturally, it's called the bluebird. But then, there are other birds you knew in Germany that don't live here. There are no storks, cuckoos, magpies, larks, nightingales, or yellowhammers. Of course, by this time most of our birds have gone south for the winter. The carndinals and woodpeckers stay around though. You might see some if you watch for them."

Christian was fascinated with all he heard and saw of the new land. Daniel seemed to know so much about it. His pleasant, friendly way of explaining and describing things was as good as hearing a story.

Before noon they came to the western fork of the Brandywine Creek. The horses forded the stream without difficulty.

"We often have trouble crossing this creek, but we have had two dry years in a row, so it is pretty shallow now," Daniel said. "In 1752 we had such an abundant harvest we had more wheat than we could get to the market. We fed it to the hogs. Now the last two years we could have used some of the surplus we had then. Perhaps next year we will have a better harvest. But the Lord has been good to us and we can't complain."

The further west they had come, the fewer clearings were to be seen. The wildlife population increased as the human population decreased. Cottontail rabbits dived off the road as the wagons passed. An almost continual stream of wildlife rippled among the trees like tiny waves at a sandy shore.

"It almost seems one could say this is a land flowing with milk and honey," Mother remarked. "With all this game, surely there is no reason for going hungry."

"A man with a mind to work won't go hungry here," Daniel agreed. "But the game is not always so plentiful. We had a very hot summer in 1738. Men dropped dead in the harvest fields and even birds died of the heat. In 1740 and '41 we had severely cold and snowy winters. There were some floods, too. A lot of the wild animals starved because their food was covered by the deep snow. It was pretty hard on those who depended on deer and turkeys for their meat."

"We don't expect to go through life without any hardships," Mother said. "If we have peace and freedom to worship and obey God according to His

Word, that is what matters most."

"Yes," Daniel agreed, "and we have always had that here. I pray God we always shall."

"We are just above the upper end of the Pequea Creek now," Daniel said a while later. "From here the creek runs southwest down to the Susquehanna River. Down there in the Pequea Valley is where the first Swissers in Lancaster County settled in 1709-10. When my father came over from Germany in 1696, he lived around Philadelphia for several years before moving to the Pequea Valley. Soon after that settlement was begun, there were others along the Conestoga and Octoraro Creeks. At first only Indians and Swissers lived in Lancaster County. And neither of them were too plentiful then."

"Are there many Indians now?" Christian asked eagerly.

"I don't know why you are so anxious to see Indians," Anna said. She sounded as though she was afraid to see them.

"We still have some Indians," Daniel answered Christian's question. "But they are gradually moving away. We have never had any trouble with them. Mostly they are Piquews (Pequeas) and a few Conestogas. In the early days, when my father first moved to the Pequea Valley, the Indians were our best neighbors. They shared liberally out of their own food supplies whenever anyone asked. We often went hunting and fishing with them. They usually lived in the meadows and scarcely more than six families were ever found at one place at a time. Their chief, Tanawa, sold his lands to William

Penn. He was at the elm in Kensington where Penn and the Indian chiefs made their Great Treaty. They have kept peace, but as the land fills up with white settlers they are leaving. I expect some day there will not be any Indians left in the whole county."

"This is Peter's Road," Daniel said as he waved good-bye to Christian Herr and Jacob Frey in the other wagon and turned north near White Horse onto a smaller road. "Now it's starting to smell like home." It was not hard to see he was eager to see his wife and family again after being away for more than a week.

"Why is this called Peter's Road?" Peter wondered.

"It was named for an old trader who often traveled this way from the Pequea to the Conestoga," Daniel explained. "He is buried along this road."

"How much further does the King's High Road go?" Mother asked.

"Only about twelve miles west to Lancaster," Daniel answered. "It branches out in two directions there. The short branch goes to Wright's Ferry.[1] Jacob will cross there to go south to York. But the road is not nearly as good as this after you cross the river. The western country beyond the Susquehanna River is pretty much unexplored territory. No one knows exactly what all lies between here and the Pacific Ocean. I heard tell of some Indians who traveled 2300 miles from Philadelphia and saw big horned sheep and deer with straight antlers. This is a big country. Pennsylvania is far from an island as some people in Germany believe it to be."

---

[1] Wrightsville

"Where does the other branch of the road go?" Ulrich wondered.

"Oh yes! I didn't say, did I?" Daniel laughed. "The longer division of the King's High Road goes north to Harris' Ferry.[1] You would cross the Susquehanna River on that ferry if you wanted to go to the Cumberland Valley, the Juniata River or Fort Du Quense[2] on the forks of the Ohio River.[3] I heard the French and Indians have been fighting together against the English at Fort Du Quense. The French turned the Indians against the English. Indian raids on English settlers are increasing. I don't like the looks of it. But so far we have not had any trouble with Indians in Earl Township. They respect men who keep their word."

Peter's Road twisted and turned, going alternately north and west. As they rounded one of the sharp bends in the road, they saw another small creek running east and west.

"This is Mill Creek. It's the last creek we cross before home," Daniel exalted as they forded the shallow water in the creek bed. "It's only a few more miles now to Groff's Thal.[4] Did you ever hear how we came to live here?"

Even if he had heard the story before, Christian would have wanted to hear it again. Daniel loved story telling and Christian loved listening. He smiled to himself as Daniel began.

"My father was one of the first settlers in the Pequea Valley, as I said before. Hans Herr's fol-

---

[1]Harrisburg
[2]Pittsburg
[3]Allegheny and Monongahela Rivers
[4]Groffdale

122

lowers bought 5000 acres from the Penns for about ten cents an acre. Penn himself sold only large tracts of land, you see. But those who bought could resell to others.

"Well, one day my father's horses ran away," Daniel continued. "He went through the Pequea Valley hunting them, but couldn't find them. He then followed the Conestoga River in a northeast direction and found the piece of land we are just coming to, which is now called Earl Township. He saw all this rich limestone land that is so good for farming. He saw that the Conestoga ran through the area for miles with plenty of power to turn the grindstones of many mills. Besides the Conestoga there were the Muddy, Mill, and Cocalico Creeks and many other smaller streams that run in every direction. It is one of the best watered and most beautiful sections of the country. My father was so impressed with what he saw that he went back to the Pequea Valley determined to buy the land in Earl Township.

"The land was surveyed several times, and it was not until 1737 that my father finally got a deed from Thomas Penn for 1419 acres. Later on it was re-surveyed and Father was granted an extra 91 acres which had been missed. Of course by this time the price was higher than when Hans Herr first bought the land. My father paid about eighteen cents an acre instead of ten cents.

"We moved to Groff's Thal long before Father actually got the deed," Daniel continued. "Our family was the first white family to live here. But it was not long until other Swissers saw what a good land it was and came too. There are two Swisser groups now; one at Groff's Thal and the other at Weber's Thal. Other Germans came as well, and some Welsh settled on a chain of hills they call the Welsh Mountains. There are about 800 people living in Earl Township today."

"Why is it called Earl Township?" Elizabeth wondered.

"My father did not call this Earl Township[1] from the beginning," Daniel said. "The people living here gave it that name in 1729 when it was organized into a township. It was their way of honoring him for being the first settler. *Earl* is the English word for *Groff.*"

The wagon rocked slightly as it bumped across and then settled into the shallow ruts of a road that ran from east to west, joining Peter's Road.

"Welcome home!" Daniel exclaimed, grinning broadly. "We are in Earl Township. Another mile or so and we will see home. How does a good, hot meal and a bed sound?"

"Wonderful!" Mother sighed. And Christian agreed wholeheartedly.

"What is this road called?" Ulrich asked.

"This is the Horseshoe Road.[2] Earltown[3] is built along this road two miles from the intersection. John Diffenderfer was the first to build a home there in 1728. It was known then as Saeue Schwamm because of the fertile black soil. The town has grown quickly and is now the biggest town in

---

[1]Earl Township was divided in 1833 into the three present-day districts of East Earl, Earl, and West Earl Townships.

[2]Route 23

[3]New Holland

124

Earl Township. I suppose you will go there to market many times after you are settled."

A short distance west, Daniel again turned north onto a small road.

"This is the home road," he announced.

A little further on the wagon crossed another narrow road.

"Down there is the mill my father built," Daniel said as he nodded toward the east. "And to the west is our Swisser burying ground. But the best place of all is just ahead. Whoa! Whoa there," he called to the horses as they stopped in front of a tidy, comfortable-looking log house.

"Father! Father!" shrieked the voice of a little form that fairly flew from the front door and flung itself into Daniel's outstretched arms.

"Anna! Have you been good while I was away?" Daniel greeted his youngest daughter.

"Oh, yes," Anna answered. "Oh, Father, I thought you would never come. It seemed like such a long time."

"You can't get rid of me that easily. I always come back. And look what I brought you this time," he teased, taking her to the wagon. "Come and say hello to our company."

Christian, who had been watching the joyful reunion of father and daughter, saw the little girl's sparkling eyes above her rosy cheeks turn shy as she seemed to become aware of the Burkholder family for the first time.

Daniel helped Mother and the girls down from the wagon as the boys swung themselves down. Little Anna properly shook hands with them all.

"Wie gehet'es,"[1] she said to each one.

When she shook Christian's hand, he grinned self-consciously and answered, "Zimlich gut,"[2] as he had learned was the proper response.

By this time, Daniel's wife, with Daniel Jr., the baby of the family, had also come out of the house to meet them. Her welcome was warm and sincere. Like Mrs. Rittenhouse in Germantown, she seemed to know just what travelers needed most. The bubbling, hot squirriel stew was served as soon as it was ready. The chunks of meat and potatoes in their thick gravy proved to be as delicious as the tantalizing aroma had promised it would be. The beds provided for them afterwards were the only other thing they could have wanted.

"What do you think, Christli?" Peter whispered as they lay down side by side on their mats on the upstairs floor.

"What do you mean?" Christian asked in return.

"Do you think you will like this place?" Peter reworded his question.

"I like it already," Christian declared stoutly. "Daniel is so nice. He is almost as good as Father. I just know we will all like living here."

---

[1]How are you?
[2]Pretty good.

Chapter 19

A House Raising

The month of November was nearly half gone. The leaves, which had been so beautiful on the two-day trip from Philadelphia, were all brown and fallen. Frequently, gray skies warned of the winter soon to begin.

Since they had arrived in Earl Township, the Burkholder family had worked hard to build a log home before winter set in. Daniel Groff had some unused acres in a nice location near the banks of the Conestoga which he was willing to rent to them. There was a grassy meadow nearby where they could cut plenty of hay for the cow they would need now and the stock they would probably add later. A clearing could soon be made for the log house and cattle shed. As they were able, other land could be cleared for fields, a garden, and the acre of flax the law required to be grown.

Daniel's brothers, Marx and Samuel, came to

help clear the land where the house would stand, and hew the fallen trees into square logs. Ulrich could swing an ax as good as any man and took his place among them. Peter and Christian worked with Daniel's son, Christian, at trimming branches from the trees and gathering stones for the foundation and fireplace. It was slow, hard work. But gradually the pile of stones and hewn timbers grew.

"We'll have you folks under roof before the snow flies," Daniel promised as work ended one day. "We will be ready to make a raising in a day or two. I think we will send out word of a raising for next week."

Word of the raising was spread rapidly by the same method that was used to announce a funeral or other special meetings. Each of the Groff brothers told his neighbor in each direction. These four neighbors told their four nearest neighbors. The chain continued until the invitation to the raising had spread to all the Swissers in the Groff's Thal and Weber's Thal districts.

Christian had never been to a raising, so he was not quite sure what to expect. But Anna and Christian Groff knew. They could hardly wait, and they made Christian eager, too, with their excitement. A raising meant a good time. People for miles around would come early in the morning, bringing tools to work with and food to eat. The children could laugh, run, and play games together since it was not a Sunday. There were plenty of babies for the girls to play with. The women brought great kettles of food to simmer and bubble over open fires at the edge of the clearing. At noon they would set long tables loaded with good food for the hard-

128

working men. The women, too, enjoyed the chance to visit and to have a change from their usual housework. It was a big social event. No one wanted to miss a gathering like this.

The walls of the house rose up rapidly as the men lifted the heavy logs and placed them one above the other. The squared logs fit together more tightly than round ones, leaving fewer and smaller cracks to be filled with chinking. In the center of the house other men built the huge fireplace. It made one whole wall of the kitchen. At one end an opening was made to the bake oven which reached back into the next room and served double duty as a heater. The huge chimney rose up through the center of the upstairs, heating the one large room there as well. The house of a German settler could easily be identified by its squared logs and central chimney. English, Scot, or Welsh settlers built their chimneys at the gable ends of the house. But Germans did not believe in wasting anything. By having a central fireplace and chimney, less heat was lost to the outside.

A cozy log house, complete with windows and a roof, stood by evening in the little clearing where only a pile of logs and stones had lain in the morning. Mother looked at it happily. The thick walls were sturdy and solid. The chinking between the logs would make it snug and warm in winter. It was very small and crude compared to what they had left behind in Gerolsheim, but it would meet their needs very well.

As the tired but happy family rode back to the Groffs home for the night, their hearts as well as the wagon were overflowing. Many of the people who had come to the raising brought gifts for the new family. There were feather ticks, homespun cloth, and tanned buckskin, as well as supplies of flour, cornmeal, molasses, candles, homemade soap, and even a cow which was tied to the back of the wagon to follow them home.

"This is just too much," Mother murmured with tears in her eyes. "We have never seen so much kindness. Why, we don't even know a lot of these people! Yet they have given us so much."

"Our people always help each other," Mrs. Groff said. "We all know how hard it is to get started in a new country. If you were given more than another new settler, it was given to honor your great courage in coming here without your husband."

A few more days were spent setting up a shelter for the cow and finishing the inside of the house. At last it was ready to move into. Christian could hardly wait for the morning of moving day. It was not that he did not like living with the Groffs. But they were all eager to be settled in their own home and begin providing for themselves. Now the heavy trunk was loaded into the wagon for the last time along with the other gifts their new friends had given them and the things they had made in Germantown.

Christian was too excited to sit still and ride in the wagon. Besides, the day was so damp and chilly he could keep warm better if he ran beside the wagon. He dug his hands deep into his pockets and bent his head against the wind that blew in his face and made his eyes water. When he could see the house, he ran ahead of the wagon and sprinted up the faint path.

At the front door he stopped. He smelled smoke. He stepped back to look up at the chimney. Yes, smoke was coming from their chimney. Someone was inside! Christian hesitated, trying to decide if he should go in or wait for the others. Just then the door swung open on its big, hammered iron hinges.

"Well, come in, come in," a hearty voice chuckled. "Don't stand out in the cold."

Christian's eyes lit up with surprise and joy as he spun around to see Daniel's brother, Marx, standing on the doorstep.

"But how did you know we were coming?" Christian gasped as the wagon stopped beside him.

"Oh, I hear things," Marx laughed. "I just thought I would get a fire going until you got here and give you a hand with that trunk."

"It was certainly thoughtful of you," Mother smiled, going into the house where a cheerful fire blazed in the huge fireplace. "You people think of everything."

The wagonload of things they had brought was soon unloaded and all was put in place. Except for the trunk, they had not brought any furniture from home. But they did not need any. The men who built the house had firmly pegged together four straight smooth slabs of wood to make a frame for a bedstead for Mother. It was set in the corner of the house and pegged solidly to the wall. A rope stretched zigzag across the bottom of it and around pegs on both sides of the frame. The one corner of the bed that was not against a wall was pegged to a tall slab of wood that reached from the floor to the ceiling above. With a straw tick to lie on and a

132

feather tick for cover, it was as comfortable as any bed made on a regular bedstead. The rest of the family could sleep on the floor of the upstairs for the present.

The kitchen table had quickly been made of two slabs of solid oak wood. One end of the slabs had been stuck in a crack in the wall and the other end rested on short, upright logs. The chairs were chunks of big logs. It was not fancy, but it would do nicely. And best of all, it was all their own.

The three boys would begin working for neighbors for wages as soon as they were settled in. There was no school to attend, and they would need all the money the boys could earn to buy supplies for the winter. The sixty-six cents the three of them together could earn for a day's labor was a little more than was needed to buy a bushel of wheat. But they would have no trouble finding work. There were plenty of farmers willing to hire help to clear land and uproot stumps. Over winter the grain would be threshed with flails on the barn floors. They would need to work harder and make do with less than they had been used to. But they were ready to do it willingly for the freedom it would mean for them. After a few good harvests, life would be easier. Then perhaps they could help other new settlers as they had been helped.

Fine, white flakes of snow were flying through the air when Christian wakened in the morning. Mother turned from stirring the mush in the pot over the fire when he and Peter came down the steps to the kitchen.

"Daniel said we would be under roof before snow

133

flies. Looks like we just made it," she said with gladness in her voice.

When the simple meal of mush, molasses, milk, and tea was finished, Mother opened Father's Bible.

"I wanted to read something special this morning," she said, looking around at the expectant faces of her six children. "I could think of nothing better than Hebrews 11."

Looking down at the page, Mother began reading in her clear, musical German of the power of faith in the lives of the ancient saints—of Abel, Enoch, Noah, and Abraham.

"By faith Abraham, when he was called to go out into a place which he should after receive for an inheritance, obeyed; and he went out, not knowing whither he went. By faith he sojourned in the land of promise, as in a strange country, dwelling in tabernacles with Isaac and Jacob, the heirs with him of the same promise: For he looked for a city which hath foundations, whose builder and maker is God."

Mother continued reading of the faith of Moses, Samuel, David and all those who had been persecuted for their faith and driven from their homes. When she finished, they all dropped to their knees and poured out their thanks and praise to God for sparing their lives in the long journey now behind them and asking His blessing on them as they began that morning the new life that lay ahead.

"I think this morning we should sing 'Nun Danket Alle Gott,'" Ulrich said when they had risen from their knees. The overflowing hearts of the seven singers joined as one as their voices blended to lift the hymn of praise to God:

134

Now thank we all our God, with hearts and hands and voices;

Who wondrous things hath done; in whom this world rejoices;

Who from our mother's arms hath blessed us on our way

With countless gifts of love, and still is ours today."

Christian sang as loudly and sincerely as his older brothers and sisters, both thanking God for His goodness in the past and asking His blessing in the future. When the hymn had ended, tears shimmered on Mother's eyelashes, but a gentle smile made her face shine. It was not the sad sort of smile she had had ever since Father became sick. It was a real smile that said her heart was happy and peaceful at last.

Chapter 20

Faith

Christian sat opposite his mother in front of the fireplace. Her needle flashed in and out as her busy hands stitched a new homespun shirt for him. He had grown so fast in the last six years she could hardly keep him in clothes. In approximately three months, he would be fifteen. His shoulders were almost as broad as a man's and he already stood head and shoulders over her. He looked so much like his father that she got a lump in her throat when she looked at him.

A big book lay open on Christian's lap. He was writing on the fly leaf. It was a *Martyrs Mirror*, printed in German at the Ephrata Cloister in 1748. Obtaining it earlier in the day had been the fulfillment of a dream which he had long cherished unspoken in his heart. The dream of owning his own Bible was not yet reality, but would come in due time.

"This martyr book belongs to me, Christian

Burkholder," he wrote in German script, "and I have bought it for my good and the salvation of my soul. In the year of Christ, one thousand, [seven hundred] and sixty-one. Anno 15 February, 1761, and it cost me one pound and 17 shillings."*

On another page he wrote the names of his brothers and sisters:

"The year 1734—Miss Barbara Burkholder
The year 1735—Miss Anna Burkholder
The year 1737—Ulrich Burkholder
The year 1740—Miss Elizabeth Burkholder
and the seventh of May 1743—Peter Burkholder
the first of June, 1746—Christian Burkholder, Jr."

Carefully, Christian blotted the ink and then asked, "And now, what shall I read, Mother?"

"Anything you like," she answered.

Christian read several accounts of the sufferings of the martyrs. At the ending of one, he fell silent and sat staring into the fire. What he had just read reminded him of some of the earliest memories he had of Grandfather Burkholder. He seemed to hear again Grandfather telling of his father's persecution in Switzerland and how the Burkholders had moved to Germany, searching for peace and freedom. From there it was only a small step to memories of his own father and how he wanted to come to Pennsylvania. He remembered Father's death and the hardships of the long ocean voyage as if they were yesterday.

Life in the last six years had not been easy. Their first harvest in 1755 had been small because it was

---

*About $4

the third consecutive year of drought. He had learned to wear homemade linen, coarse homespun cloth of flax, and moccasins of deerskin. There were only candles for light, bare wooden and dirt floors, and whitewashed walls inside the house. Wooden platters and spoons, pewter dishes and mugs served them rather than china and pottery. Mother and the girls had to work in the fields and take responsibilities often left to men.

The fighting over territory which had broken out between the French and English about the same time as the Burkholders had arrived had developed into the French and Indian War, and still raged. Although no one had actually been killed by Indians in Earl Township, fear and emotions ran high. Many of the inhabitants who were not nonresistant Swissers carried guns in their harvest fields in the event they wanted to defend themselves. How long the fighting would go on and what the outcome would be, no one could tell.

Christian could not help wondering sometimes if they were really any better off than they had been in Germany. Father had wanted to come here to avoid the constant wars. And yet, there had been war ever since they had arrived. They had given all they had to come here to find peace and freedom. Had they found it? In the bottom of his heart he knew they had. Though there were constant wars and rumors of wars, Jesus said not to be troubled by them for they must precede His coming. The standard of living was different from what he remembered in Gerolsheim, but it was not worse. More difficult in a way, perhaps, but yet easier in other ways.

Now they were free to choose their occupation, which was unheard of in Germany. They could marry and pass on inheritances without paying a huge tax. They could bury their dead anywhere they chose. And best of all, neither the government nor the general public bothered their worship or ridiculed their practices. They cared little whether a man worshiped five times a day or not at all. Only a small tax was levied on the non-associators to excuse them from military duty. The great gain of this freedom more than made up for the few physical comforts they left behind in Gerolsheim.

Christian's heart welled up with gratitude to God for this good land, where he now felt at home, and to his mother who was willing to risk her life to come to it. In his own heart he resolved to be as faithful to his Lord as were the generations of Burkholders before him so that the generations to follow might have the same faith and peace he was enjoying.

Mother looked up from her sewing as the silence lengthened. She saw Christian was deep in thought.

"Christli, are you tired of reading?" she asked gently after a time.

The firelight flickered over his face as he looked up and ran his hand through his bushy hair.

"Oh, no. Just thinking," he answered seriously. "Mother, it must have been very hard for you to leave the old country and come here. Maybe it was even more difficult for you to be faithful in life than it was for the martyrs to be faithful in death. But I'm so glad you did it. And I can only pray I will be as faithful as you if God asks me to do something hard."

"The God who stood by the martyrs in death and by me in life is still the same God, Christli," Mother reminded him. "My life has not been easy, but God has never failed me. Only He knows what your life will be. If you trust Him, He will never fail you."

Christian looked down again at the big book in his lap, seeking the place where he had left off reading. He knew Mother was right, as usual. They were not rich in the things the world recognized as valuable. Yet they were extremely wealthy. The hidden riches of faith deep in their hearts was more than enough to see them safely through this life and into the next. With the feedom of worship they now enjoyed, the possibilities for increasing this hidden store of riches was unlimited.

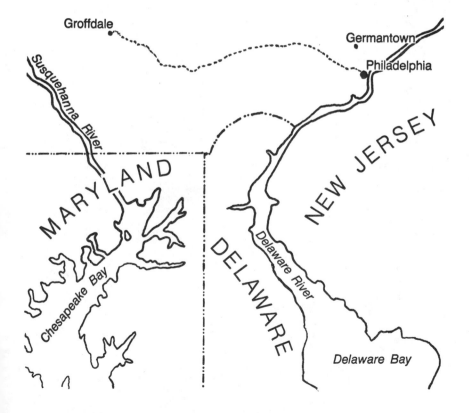

PENNSYLVANIA

NEW JERSEY

Delaware River

Groffdale

Germantown

Philadelphia

Susquehanna River

MARYLAND

NEW JERSEY

Chesapeake Bay

DELAWARE

Delaware River

Delaware Bay

N

Cowes
Rotterdam
Gerolsheim
Philadelphia
Atlantic Ocean
N

Epilogue

Christian Burkholder Jr. became a strong Mennonite leader in northern Lancaster County. He was ordained to the ministry on August 12, 1770 at 24 years of age. Eight years later, on October 18, 1778, he was ordained bishop of the Groffdale-Weaverland district of the Mennonite Church. He faithfully and capably performed the duties of this office for nearly 31 years until his death on May 13, 1809 at 63 years of age. He was said to be a powerful preacher whose audience was attentive to his sermons.

Christian Burkholder is best known for his booklet, *Anrede an die Jugend (Address to Youth)*, which he wrote in 1792. It was signed by twenty-seven ministers and deacons, making it an official document of the Mennonite Church. It was first printed in 1804 and reprinted in 1829, 1868, and 1873 in German as an independent book. The *Anrede* was translated into English in 1857. It was published as part of the *Spiritual Conversation of Saving Faith* which was reprinted seven times. The most recent reprinting was done in 1974. That this writing could have survived nearly two hundred years is itself a proof of the greatness of the work. It is still in print in both German and English.

Christian married Anna Groff, daughter of Daniel Groff, on July 13, 1766, when he had just passed his twentieth birthday. They had nine children.

In addition to being a leader in church affairs, Christian was also a leader in agriculture. From his father-in-law he acquired several farms along the Conestoga Creek, lying south and west of Fiands Mill Bridge. The home farm is now owned by Paul Z. Martin, an eighth-generation descendant. When Christian retired, his son, Christian Jr., took over the home farm. Two and one-half acres were reserved for Christian's two unmarried daughters, Anna and Elizabeth. It is believed Christian lived his last years with these two daughters in a log house that was on the acreage south of the Conestoga but east of the Fiands Mill Bridge. The quaint old log house was torn down about 1860.

Christian was buried beside his wife in the beautiful Groffdale Mennonite Cemetery. Their graves are adequately marked by red sandstone markers, a type rather uncommon in the grave yard. The original site of the cemetery and the first church building (built in 1755) is where the brick Groffdale Church is now located.

Christian's mother lived in Pennsylvania forty-one years. The record in Christian's *Martyrs Mirror,* tells us she died while at his home on November 13, 1795. She was also buried in the Groffdale cemetery near Christian and his wife. All the Burkholders in the U.S. and Canada who descended from the children of this widow owe her an unpayable debt of gratitude for her bravery in undertaking the long and dangerous voyage to Pennsylvania. Her faith in spite of hardship and suffering has resulted in great blessing to us.

Nothing is known of the descendants of the sisters of Christian Burkholder. Perhaps traces can be found as genealogists continue to search.

Ulrich married and lived on a farm near the present village of Bowmansville, Pennsylvania. The farm is presently owned by William Musser who also has the Burkholder deeds descending from Ulrich. Ulrich was a plain and blunt-speaking minister of the Bowmansville (or Muddy Creek, as it was then called) Church. He has a large group of Burkholder descendants who are now in Ontario, Canada. Also, there are numerous Borkholter Amish families in Ohio and Indiana that claim lineage to Ulrich Burkholder.

Peter Burkholder married Margaret Huber, daughter of John Huber of New Holland. In 1790 they joined the Mennonite exodus to the Shenandoah Valley in Virginia and located near Broadway. They had four sons and four daughters who have many descendants today, mostly in Virginia. The best known of their sons was Peter Jr. who became a Mennonite bishop and wrote several devotional books. The church met for some time in their house and later built the "Burkholder Church," which has long since been called Weavers Church. In 1798, Peter Sr.'s wife, Margaret, died and was buried in Trissels Mennonite Cemetery. The next year Peter visited his brother, Christian, in Lancaster County with his brother-in-law, John Huber, as a traveling companion. During the visit, Peter died and was buried in the Groffdale Mennonite Cemetery near his mother.